JOSÉ LUIS CUEVAS

JOSÉ LUIS CUEVAS

SELF-PORTRAIT WITH MODEL

Introduction: JOSÉ GÓMEZ-SICRE
Letters: JOSÉ LUIS CUEVAS

One hundred and five drawings
reproduced full-size

RIZZOLI
NEW YORK

Published in the United States
of America in 1983 by:

RIZZOLI INTERNATIONAL PUBLICATIONS, INC.
712 Fifth Avenue/New York 10019

Copyright © Ediciones Polígrafa, S. A. 1983

Translation by Kenneth Lyons

Library Congress Catalog Card Number: 83-42605
ISBN: 0-8478-0489-5

Printed in Spain by La Polígrafa, S. A.
Parets del Vallès (Barcelona)
Dep. Leg.: B. 3.044 - 1983

CONTENTS

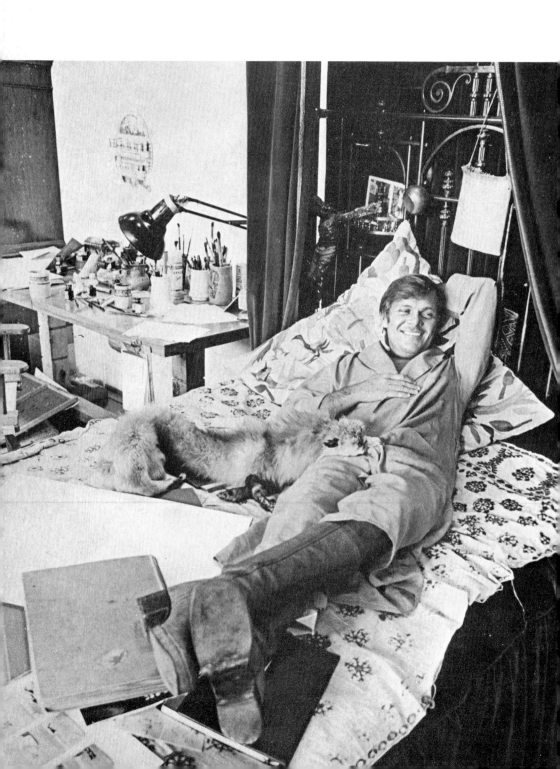

Just as I was starting work on this text, in the early morning of October 5th in the appalling year of 1981, I had a telephone call from a friend in Mexico City to tell me the great news: José Luis Cuevas had been awarded the National Prize for Culture. Thus I realized that not everything had gone so badly in the ten months we had been living in the midst of bomb attacks, invasions, betrayals, justifications of fraud, unnecessary deaths, the exaltation of truculence and the prosperity of the wicked. For nations that called themselves independent and democratic had been serving the cause of injustice and totalitarian ambition. In the cause of treason, too, and armed with the spirit of betrayal, they had seemed to triumph over right and honesty.

All the nausea I was feeling, the disgust with which I observed the most contemptible side of human behavior all over the world in our time, was assuaged and dissipated when I heard of Cuevas' triumph.

In the very land where he had been born and brought up, and where he had also been most reviled, justice had finally been done to him. All I could think of saying, before I hung up, was: "At last Cuevas has been recognized in Mexico!"

Awarded by a committee of Mexicans, and with funds from the Mexican State, this prize is a fitting recompense for the contribution that this much attacked and controversial — though apolitical — citizen has made to the culture of his country and to its prestige in the rest of the world.

Cuevas had no need to enter any political party that would shelter him under its demagogic mantle. On the contrary, indeed, he has received little but insults and obloquy. He has been threatened, and not long ago his house was even machine-gunned. The fact is that those who envy his fame and creative talent cannot bear to see him go on living, triumphing and, above all, working with ever greater energy and assurance. Nothing affronts the mediocre so much as the success of those who deserve to succeed. As if this were not enough, very soon now (in the early months of the coming year) he is due to receive international homage. Over a dozen exhibitions of his work are to be opened simultaneously in different parts of America and Europe. The cinema, the television and the radio will all combine to pay him tribute — as will this book that I have now sat down to write in the panegyrical tone induced by an event that I thought would never come about, at least in whatever lifetime is left to me: José Luis Cuevas winning the National Prize of Mexico!

It is in Barcelona, far away in Spain, that they are going to print this book about the artist and his relationship with that same unforgettable Mediterranean town. It was I who first introduced José Luis to Barcelona, some twenty years ago now. Since we had forgotten to book rooms, we found ourselves in a city packed with visitors, but by resorting to a little modest bribery we managed to get two tiny rooms in an hotel which, as in a fairy tale, has since vanished. It seemed simply to be wiped off the face of the city, and no amount of curiosity has enabled us to locate it again. However, it saved us from spending the night on a bench in the Ramblas or trundling back to Castile on a milk train. A Catalan's "No" is as unequivocal as an Englishman's, so when they told us there was not a room to be had in the city we knew that they meant what they said. The morning light brought comfort, but we still had to move to a different hotel every day (ending up at the Ritz). That week we had planned to spend visiting museums and studying Gaudí at first hand. The Güell Park and the Casa Milà ("La Pedrera") were wonderful discoveries, and José Luis was fascinated by Gaudí's Church of the Holy Family. He also greatly enjoyed the Catalan Romanesque art we saw. I remember, too, visiting one of the museums in the center of the city, where we saw an extraordinary collection of portrait drawings by Ramon Casas, the forerunner of Picasso who, together with Isidre Nonell, was largely responsible for introducing the young artist from Málaga (who finally became thoroughly Catalanized) to the new trends in art. In the same museum we saw some works by Fortuny, still a great artist for the present generation and perhaps for ever. In the Gothic Quarter, José Luis was greatly impressed by the old Catalan sculptures in the Museo Marés. Then, as now, he always carried a little sketch-book in his pocket, and in that museum he made quite a few sketches of those hieratic virgins carved by the medieval image makers of Catalonia.

We used to love strolling down the Rambla de las Flores, or visiting the old fishermen's quarter of the Barceloneta, with all its restaurants along the beach; I also induced José Luis to try the bold, simple cooking of the Caracoles restaurant in the Carrer Escudillers. We enjoyed that week to the full, but we have never been back to Barcelona together. Each of us has often returned alone, and I know that he adores the grandeur of the place, but it is only now that we have begun to retrace in memory those wanderings of ours through one of the most beautiful cities in Europe, a city where both he and I would be delighted to live. Since neither of us has any relatives left in Catalonia, this wish is quite gratuitous, motivated only by attractions which may be dissimilar for one and the other.

Both José Luis Cuevas and I, however, do have Catalan ancestry. His maternal grandmother, Felicia Carbonell i Llensa, was born in Blanes, then a little fishing village. From there the family emigrated to Sagua la Grande, in the northern central region of Cuba, but when the War of Independence (later to develop into the Spanish American War) broke out in 1895, they moved to the part of Mexico nearest to Cuba, where they settled in the city of Mérida, capital of Yucatán State.

What the artist chiefly remembers about his grandmother is that she was always concerned about her grandson's precarious health, though without any sentimentality. "I was just a grandson," José Luis once told me, "whose premature death it was her grandmotherly duty to prevent. My maternal grandmother, in fact, was of a steely character poles apart from that of her grandson, a dull boy who spent all his time playing with pieces of charcoal or stubs of pencils, with which he would scrawl all over any paper that came into his hands. I was always well provided with paper by the maids, who, with that innate kindness characteristic of simple folk, seemed to have no other aim but to spoil me — or, if you like, to make my childhood a pleasant one. This they certainly succeeded in doing, at least as regards the enthusiasm with which they would bring me every stray piece of paper, sometimes thrown away and trodden on, that they found on the floor in my grandfather's paper mill, in the flat over which I was born."

Indeed his grandfather's paper mill was an important factor in his early training. This mill produced different qualities of paper, ranging from one like newsprint, which was sold in huge reels, to tissue paper, the soft kind they use for wrapping in shops, or Manila paper with its rough, raw ochre color. José Luis accepted them all, almost indistinctly. He was just as happy using a piece of cardboard bearing the footprints of the workers as scraps of veiny antique or the smoother bond, either of them asking to be drawn on. The only ones he could not stand were glossy papers, whatever their weight or density. He disliked the lightness with which the charcoal or pencil ran over those shiny surfaces. I have always thought that this tactile antagonism that made no resistance to the hand ranging avidly over surfaces was largely responsible for the assurance, dynamism and strength of his line from that very early age when he first began to create forms.

Today the artist still draws on any drawable surface he finds to hand. He has frequently used the paper napkins in cafés — later treasured by the friends who were with him at the time — to develop ideas. Even on the edges of tables, on marble or any other material, he has sometimes left exquisitely finished drawings of characters. On matchboxes too, both inside or outside; when he is telephoning, on the pages and covers of the directory or on his friends' and relatives' telephone pads he has left these traces of his art. When he has nothing better than a burnt-out match in his hand, he is apt to rub it vigorously over the nearest surface; if he has no substance at all that will leave a visual trace, he will resort to the furrows he can make with his fingernails. His urge to create is irrepressible, and it becomes compulsive when he is confronted with a ream of paper.

This book is, in principle, the result of that obsessive attitude. In 1980 José Luis was visiting a shop in Barcelona specializing in artist's materials, where they made him a present of a sample-book of high-quality papers. It had just a hundred pages, amounting to as many challenges to a restless hand that is always seeking to express something in line. That was how the whole process of this book began. Somebody, apparently, bet him that it would take him a month to fill all those pages, to which the artist retorted: "I can do it in one day without spoiling a sheet. All on the same theme, besides, and without repeating myself once." There are precedents for this adventurous attitude of Cuevas which show his sporting readiness to compete with his work. I remember, for instance, the case of the open passage that was all that could be seen from my basement office with a wall finished in white paint, very deeply textured. The chief painter of the buildings came to my office one day to show me a new synthetic substance which was supposed to be tested in outdoor conditions. He asked me if I knew anybody who would like to try it, but added that he could only supply it in black and white. On hearing this José Luis, who happened to be present, at once took off his jacket, went out to the passage and began to decorate the wall with a large-scale figure. He asked us to time him; it was then four o'clock in the afternoon. There were several of us watching. When the drawing was absolutely finished from any professional point of view, he signed it and asked the time again; only thirty minutes had elapsed. He had more than met the challenge he had offered himself. The figure is still there, only slightly deteriorated after all these years and defying time under the rain, snow and perpetual damp of Washington, in a corner hardly ever visited by the sun. Also in the nature of a wager was the famous "ephemeral" mural he painted on several square yards of paper, with the stretcher set up on the flat roof of a house in Mexico City's Zona Rosa. He did this whole mural in a matter of minutes, and when he had finished he tore it to pieces, despite the protesting shouts from the crowd that had gathered in the street below. As the artist has said in public, he did this to show the indifference he felt to Mexican mural painting. This was, in fact, the first step in his career against established art, his first appearance in the role of David with his sling ready.

Such strokes of daring, prompted by his complete assurance and real creative power, have all that character of unpremeditated audacity with which he sets out to win the notoriety that attracts him so much, but which he does not really need at all. The fact is that it is by now almost traditional in Mexico for artists to go for such publicity. There was the twin phenomenon of Diego Rivera and David Alfaro Siqueiros and after them have come others exploiting various systems of self-promotion that have become almost an unavoidable feature of the country's art scene.

Born into the art of his own country, José Luis Cuevas thus found himself compelled to wage the eternal war of the generations against a national establishment, so to speak, which had laid down a single system of working — murals — and a single formula — political content or message. It is natural enough that his first confrontation should have been with those who controlled that establishment. Once imposed, the system and the formula would only deteriorate, as is the inexorable fate of all cultural movements. Cuevas' fight against the art "authorities" opened the eyes of his own generation and the following one, both hitherto intimidated by what amounted to political blackmail. The only artist of any merit to have objected to the situation before was Rufino Tamayo, who was never able to give his protests that vitality which his younger colleague had enough to spare. But Cuevas used the same tactics as his adversaries, the erstwhile masters of the situation, and was soon victorious. Time, moreover, was on his side. Before long his importance could be estimated by the numbers of those opposed to him. I think this is the most outstanding service Cuevas has rendered to the culture of his country: sifting all the characters, as it were, and getting rid of the superfluous. There are many beneficiaries today, people who have had greater opportunities thanks to his action; and yet some of these are also against him, eagerly hoping to take over the position of prestige now occupied by Cuevas in his own country and abroad. Their reaction to his continuing importance in the international world of drawing and the graphic arts is one of resentment. They still regard Cuevas as a dangerously brilliant young fellow, despite the fact that he is now approaching the age of fifty and is, in fact, a mature man who is beginning to receive the rewards of the long and bitter fight in which he bravely involved himself before he was properly out of his adolescence.

It has not been easy to overcome this resentment, which is largely the result of the envy provoked by his success, by the very high quality of his work, which many people found surprising in view of the almost childish appearance of the artist. There are some elements in the human spirit that no amount of civilization can eradicate, envy is one of them. Every world of professionals or creative artists inevitably contains a high percentage of mediocrity mixing with the really worthwhile. The mediocre will use all sorts of weapons to bring down the true, original artists. But there is one factor always against them: time. This is what will determine what is to endure because of its genuine quality, the permanence of work that is done with all the rigor demanded by unchanging canons of excellence.

Cuevas' earlier work (between 1942 and 1955) shows us a vast panorama of exploration of reality; we can already see an artist who knows where he is going and how, though he does not yet know why. It is work of the instinct. The line is firm and solid, but it has not yet been set free to search for an expression per se. He knows that there is a possibility of recreating the real life around him, just as he knew — at the age of eight — how to find in the family's cat the first liberated subject in his career. To maintain that interest he used all the heterogeneous elements that pullulated in the streets around the Callejón del Triunfo, where he spent his childhood. The local beggars, the family servants, the little clay figures you could buy for a few cents in the nearest market, all of these took their place in his mind's eye and were then recreated in pieces of colored paper, accidental snippings gleaned from the cutters in his grandfather's paper mill.

The "off-limits" reality, as we might describe the period when José Luis had to go to school every day and venture into the perilous paths of a district of dubious respectability, brought him into touch with a more promiscuous section of society, the very sordidness of which held an inexplicable attraction for him. This too was recorded, though forbidden by the standards of a family with a belief in austerity. Though still a child, he was attracted by anything in the nature of strangeness, depravity or scatology. Thus his repertoire of themes from real life included fortune tellers and spiritualists, like some new Mexican version of the Spanish gypsy theme. He drew hawkers with their varied goods, beggars and people wounded or dead in the streets. Finally there are the prostitutes, excluded from any social consideration and reduced to abjection: pitiful grotesques that the audacious urchin glimpsed through shutters he was barely tall enough to reach, in broad daylight, when those poor women were engaged in activities quite different from those that gave them their livelihood.

This period, full of realistic but not obscene subjects, is characterized by strong, continuous lines, denser at the beginning than later on. It is a line rather like that of gestural painting, as in Orozco, the principal influence detected in these early works. In these drawings Cuevas seems to be attempting not so much to find their specific linear value as to leave a record of what he has seen. However, he produced a collection of drawings of high quality, in which we can clearly see his intention to take the line to extremes not often found in artists of his age.

Gradually his dialectic instrument, line as a pure value, produced ascendent variations in his work that increasingly revealed the hand and mind of a master. Above all when he did series — various works to round off a single theme: *Funeral of a Dictator, Conquest of Mexico, The Woman Painter, Charenton, Lo Spagnoletto's Bearded Woman, Homage to Quevedo* and others. There is, however, one obsessive theme, that of the self-portrait, which we find inserted in the others, an obligatory background, an ectoplasm or goblin that accompanies him everywhere and always seizes for itself some fragment of the paper, however small. José Luis achieves a transfiguration at times in these acts of usurpation with himself, which he commits as often as possible. Self-worshipping or narcissism? His own explanation is that this constant self-portraying expresses his horror of death, of the total disappearance of matter and the form given. Though I do not altogether believe it, this explanation may be at least truthful. But I think that this habit comes from his desire to show all the people who disparaged his work before, and the few left who still do so, that he has triumphed in spite of everything and that he must now be regarded, and tacitly accepted, as a king. At all events, independently of whether the correct interpretation is his or mine, these self-portraits are delightful, rather like impudent goblins that have gate-crashed his compositions and become their leitmotivs.

The hundred and five drawings produced in a single session in response to the challenge of a sample-book of fine paper, contains only a self-portrait and a female nude. It was this feat, which took him less than twenty-four hours to accomplish without spoiling a single sheet, that led to the publication of this book.

His urge to draw, as I said before, leads him to use any and every instrument that will leave traces on a surface. But of all the materials he uses to give form to the sometimes frightening fruits of his imagination, his favorites have always been simply paper, pen and ink. Paper holds a fascination for Cuevas that goes back to the very earliest years of his life. It was in his grandfather's paper mill that he first became addicted to work on this medium. But until recently the paper he normally used was of poor quality. When he was no longer living in the flat over the paper mill, his constant supply from that source stopped and he had to acquire his paper from the local stationers. His pocket-money as a child and has an adolescent was a pittance, the only paper on which he could afford to practice or perform with ink, graphite or charcoal was the sort that would not cost more than five Mexican cents a sheet. Even when he had begun to sell some of his work he was wary of trying expensive papers. As a young man he continued to observe these thrifty habits with regard to materials, and whenever any of his richer colleagues made him a present of a sheet of European paper, he hardly knew how to deal with it. His repeated attempts at drawing would utterly ruin the elegant surface and the whole thing would end up in the wastepaper basket, leaving poor Cuevas feeling defeated and frustrated. With time he has recovered his assurance in working with high-quality materials. For over ten years now his drawings have been done on the definitive support of very heavy linen rag paper.

Any recent drawing by Cuevas, especially those on a larger scale, has all the impressiveness of a work done on much more durable material than paper. In his hands, moreover, the paper becomes transformed into a document with aspirations to eternity, as an intrinsic work of art, something just as valuable as the most enduring or luxurious of materials. Besides, it is absolutely timeless. I have always said that the ancestry of his art goes back to Hieronymus Bosch, through Rembrandt, Brueghel and Grünewald (especially in the Isenheim altar-piece), as if to show that he has lingered at every stage of expressionism in the history of art. Sometimes, when he decides to curb this expressionism, his hand is attracted to the serenity of the Italian Renaissance masters. He then produces little gems that might have been signed by Leonardo, Raphael, Mantegna or any other of the great artists who offered him an example to follow whenever doubts or temperament led him to change his course. But I certainly do not wish to imply that Cuevas is simply a sponge for other artists' influences, a living lesson of art history.

In these hundred and five drawings, poured on to the paper like gifts from some particularly lavish horn of plenty, we can see the legitimacy of the painter's own expressionism, valid precisely because it neither disowns its origins nor conceals its various starting points. At his present stage of development, the maturity of a personality universally admired, he has not only thoroughly assimilated the lessons of the past and thereby enriched his creative potential, but has also continued absorbing attitudes and styles: for we find Goya and Picasso too, as evidence of the Spanish heritage working in this Mexican artist who has attained such celebrity.

The most important feature of his work, after the influence of all the great names from the remote and recent past, is the insertion of the perpetual values of the aboriginal art of his own people: the archaic, hieratic strength of pre-Columbian sculpture, with its unshakable solemnity and unerring interplay of volumes from which Cuevas' most recent work takes its strange solidity. When Cuevas draws a volume it gives the impression of flint, a dense, weighty mass described by his line with its variant values. Some of his imitators, copying the external, produce an idea of inflation and air. Where Cuevas in his line holds flesh or granite, the others trace globes of frail skin that can be inflated or deflated, flabby bladders that might at most sail a few yards in the air. Cuevas' volumes do not rise; they remain in thrall to the law of gravity and rest on the ground, with a weight similar to that of pyramids, sphinxes or tanks, all made by man, or even rolling hills or mountains, made by God. Even when the line becomes nimble and restless, and a figure rises, dances or climbs, the volumes neither become hollow nor escape into the air. In this the artist's work majestically accepts responsibility and rejects fragility. It is because of these characteristics that I have always believed in the unfading value of his work which has evolved continuously in over forty years spent perfecting his vision and his draughtsman's skill.

This series, without tedious repetitions, only consists of a female nude and a self-portrait. In their evolution both characters change in aspect but not in physiognomy. They are the artist's plastic children, constantly adopting varying expressions and poses, and accepting the most daring differences in the technique within which he conceives them. The really important factor —the line— is an instrument of purity that few contemporary artists can use so lavishly without ever for a moment losing an atom of its dash; all the virtuosity that Cuevas may display by pure experimenting in his graphic language, is incorporated into the context of his work by the immanent unity of his expression, the cohesion of his creative concept. I would say that both in drawing and in the graphic arts José Luis Cuevas is perhaps the most significant personality in the art world today.

Since the two characters that are the basis for this book bear no message and have no literary content whatsoever, on this occasion — as on others when he has been confronted with a theme in books, portfolios or print series — Cuevas does not illustrate, does not narrate, does not tell any stories; he simply draws his theme and immortalizes it as drawing, without attempting to go beyond its plastic significance, an aesthetic value that will always be the motive power of his work.

It is thanks to the stimuli of Barcelona, the paper sample-book and this protean couple that this book has been conceived and has taken shape, to become yet another living being in this repertoire of desolate humanity that Cuevas has always endeavored to present. Here, then, is the book itself, another witness to the genius of a true creative artist who has developed thanks to the bilateral culture of Mexico. This artist also possesses to a high degree the ultimate essence of that Spanish — in this case Catalan — heritage that has helped him develop to the full maturity of a career that is exemplary in Latin America. Cuevas has also been important in this aspect, for his positive values have done much to gain credit for a true international movement, the one that is taking place in the Spanish American countries, though still belittled today by the great commercial art centres, in much the same way as when the rest of the world conspired to invent a black legend for Spain.

José Gómez-Sicre
Curator of the Museum of Contemporary Art of Latin America
Organization of American States, Washington.

DRAWINGS WITH AUTOGRAPHIC LETTERS
Testing papers Nos. 1 to 22

Testing papers. 1

Barcelona, 27th April 1981

Dear Juan:

Perhaps because I was born in a paper mill and pencil factory (El lápiz del águila), paper has always had a great fascination for me.

I like trying them all, experimenting with their different textures.

There is a lot that is sensual in this playing with papers.

In paper stores I like running my fingers over the loose sheets, big or small, and it fills me with such rapture and ecstasy that anyone would think I was stroking some woman's skin.

Self-portrait with woman (as Modigliani)

Testing papers. 2

Barcelona, 27th April 1981

Sometimes you don't need to touch a paper; you don't
even need to drive a pencil over its surface. You only
have to look at it, to know what it's capable of. With
some papers you can establish a relationship straight
away.

Impatience takes hold of you. You wish you could
have it in the studio already, to use it, to rape it.

Self-portrait with woman (as Picasso)

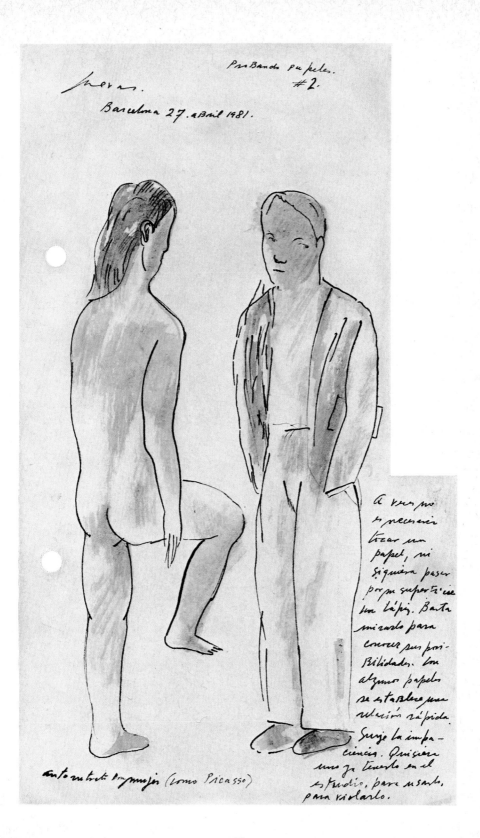

Testing papers. 3

Barcelona, 27th April 1981

Paper goes with me wherever I go. It is my most
faithful companion.

In notebooks (I always try to get the ones that have
many sheets) I constantly take notes of anything that
attracts my attention in the places I visit.

I draw very quickly, and I have developed a capacity
for not even having to see the surface I am drawing
on. I look at the model and my hand moves of its
own accord, without any guidance from the eye. That
hand knows where it has to go.

Self-portrait with woman (as Lord Byron)

Testing papers. 4

Barcelona, 27th April 1981

The papers are raped by me with everything I have
within reach: wooden matchsticks, one of those little
Chinese toothpicks children play with, any old pencil,
a pen-nib, a paintbrush dipped in ink that's been
thickened with gum arabic, and so on.

Today in Barcelona I have begun these trials on my
papers, and in my hotel room, or walking along the
docks, or in the Gothic Quarter, I have used them.

There are some papers that make me think of other
artists who have.

Self-portrait with woman (as Casanova)

Testing papers. 5

used them, and that is why I sometimes like to do
drawings "in the manner of" Goya, or Rembrandt, or
Ingres, or whoever it may be, imagining that those
papers belong to them.

At times, too, there are papers that make me think of
writers — a sheet of gilded paper, for instance, might
start me fancying that it would be just the sort for
Casanova to write his memoirs on. Then, again, a
sheet of smooth, white paper I associate with de Sade,
Lord knows why!

Self-portrait with woman (as Goya)

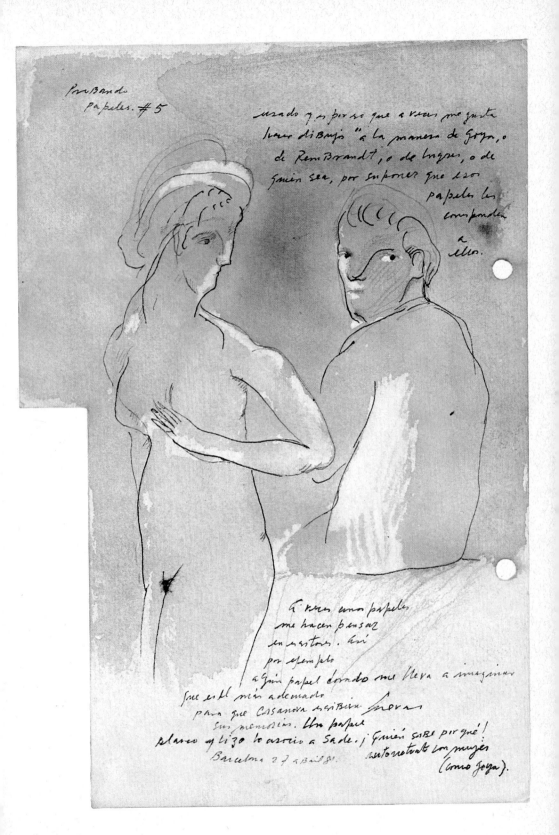

Testing papers. 6

Barcelona, 27th April 1981

There are papers that imitate the texture of a canvas.

Working on these I imagine myself as a painter, and
the way I stain them is very "pictorial." Canvas in
itself has never attracted me, though I have used it
for large-format drawings when I have had no sheets
of paper to hand on a sufficiently lavish scale. But I
find the surface of canvas inimical to me.

I even feel a sort of physical malaise when I move a
paintbrush, a pencil or a pen over a canvas.
Undoubtedly, paper is the best stuff of all for an artist
as sensuous as I am.

Self-portrait with woman (as Rembrandt)

Hay papeles que imitan la textura del lienzo.
Sobre ellos me imagino pintor y los mancho
muy "pictóricamente". El lienzo en sí nunca me
ha atraído. Lo he usado para dibujos de gran
formato, cuando no he tenido a mi alcance hojas
de papel de tamaño generoso. Pero la superficie
del lienzo es para mí re-
chazante.

Me produce
incluso una molestia
física cuando
paso por el lienzo
un pincel, una
lápiz ó una
pluma. El
papel defi-
nitivamente
mí adecua-
do para
un artista
tan sensual
como soy yo.

Nieras

autorretrato con
mujer
(como Rembrandt.)

Barcelona, 27 abril 1981.

Vicente Rojo
Ortega 298.   Tel. 228.62.95 y 2.82.14.48

Probando
papeles
#6

Testing papers. 7

Barcelona, 27th April 1981

I began to use paper when I was a very small boy, as I have already said in my precocious autobiography, *Cuevas por Cuevas*. How many sheets of paper can I have covered with my scrawls in all these years I've been drawing? Impossible to calculate. Just imagine that ever since I was a very small boy not a day has passed without having used paper to draw on. Not all the papers drawn by me have been kept. Most of them have been destroyed and thrown into the dustbin.

Self-portrait (as Ingres)

Procesando papeles · #7

Empecé a usar el papel desde muy pequeño. Ya lo
dije en mi autobiografía precoz "Cuevas por Cuevas".

¿ Cuántas hojas de pa-
pel habré sca-
raBajeado en los años
que llevo diBujando?
Imposible calcularlo.
Imaginar que desde
que yo era muy pe-
queño no ha pasa-
do día sin
que yo haya hecho
uso del papel
para diBujarlo.

No todos los
papeles di-
Bujados,
por mí
se conser-
van.

La
mayo-
ría de
ellos
son
destrui-
dos
y tira-
dos
al
Bote
de la Basura.

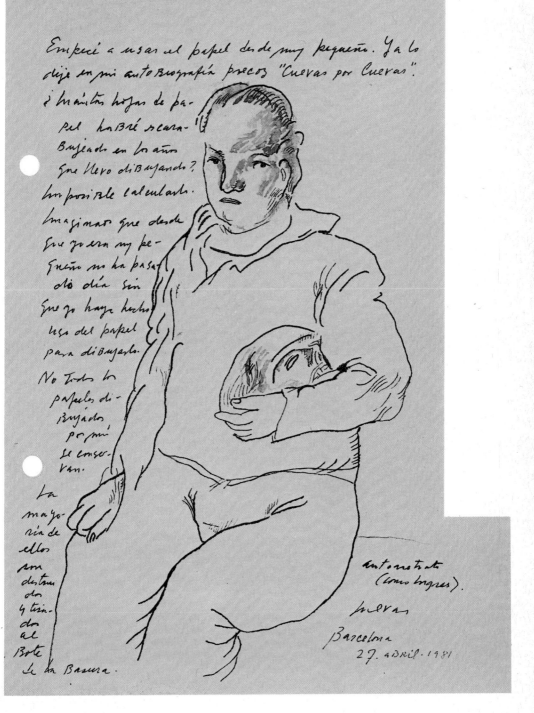

Autorretrato
(como Ingres).

Cuevas
Barcelona
27. aBril. 1981

33

Testing papers. 8

Barcelona, 27th April 1981

It has sometimes happened that I have found myself
without any paper, my stock used up by what I did
the day before — which was undoubtedly a day of
feverish activity, but which has now left me without
so much as one miserable sheet of paper to draw on.
If this happens to me in a hotel I can always resort to
using the writing paper it provides for its guests, and
on that I immediately start to draw. Those who know
me well are familiar with my practice of drawing at
every moment of the day: when I am chatting to
somebody on the phone (I have an impressive
collection of drawings done on those occasions), while
I am giving lectures, when I am eating at a restaurant.

Self-portrait with woman (as Van Gogh)

8

Me ha sucedido
en alguna ocasión encontrar-
me sin papeles. Mis reservas se
han agotado el día anterior, que
fué sin duda de trabajo febril y heme
aquí sin una miserable
hoja para trazar un dibujo.
Si esto me sucede en un ~~hotel~~ hotel
me queda el recurso de
usar las hojas que suelen
tener para
los clientes.

En tu retrato
con pipa
(como Van Gogh).

Probando papel.
8

y entonces me lanzo a dibujar en ellas. Quien me
conocen bien saben
que dibujo en todo
momento:
mientras
charlo en
el teléfono
(tengo una
impresionante
colección de di-
bujos hechos
en esas ocasiones)
mientras doy
conferencias o
como en los restau-
rantes.

Grovas

Barcelona
27 abril
1981.

35

Testing papers. 9

Barcelona, 27th April 1981

Whenever I am reading I draw at the same time in a
little notebook that is always with me during reading
sessions, and the drawings I do allude to whatever the
text is telling me. Paper is a positive vice with me. If I
couldn't get enough of it I'd go mad. I'd be quite
capable of rushing out into the street and robbing
some schoolboy of the exercise books in his satchel.
Without a stock of paper beside me I feel alone,
insecure.

On one occasion I found myself in a foreign country,
and the only paper I had for drawing on was the
unstamped pages in my passport. In my craving for
drawing paper

Self-portrait with woman (as the Marquis de Sade)

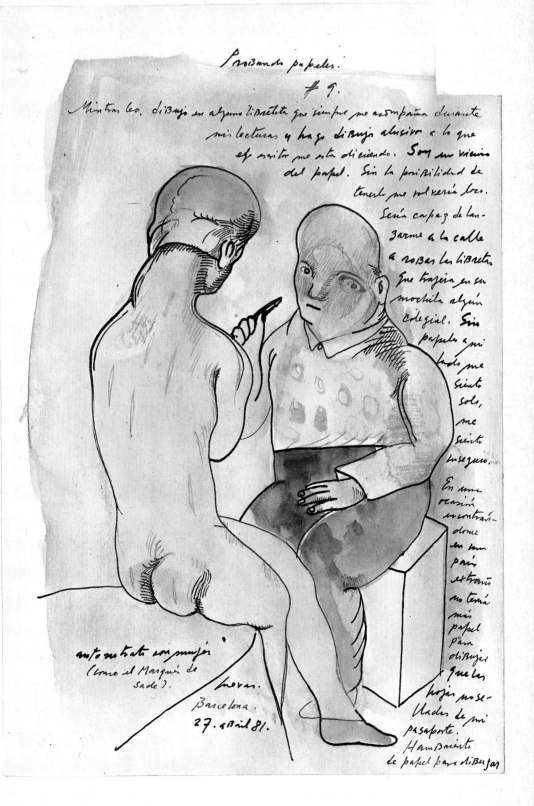

Probando papeles.

#9

Mientras leo, dibujo en alguna libretita que siempre me acompaña durante mis lecturas y hago dibujos alusivos a lo que el escrito me está diciendo. Soy un vicioso del papel. Sin la posibilidad de tenerlo me volvería loco.

Sería capaz de lanzarme a la calle a robar las libretas que trajera en su mochila algún colegial. Sin papeles a mi lado me siento solo, me siento inseguro.

En una ocasión encontrándome en un país extraño no tenía más papel para dibujar que las hojas no selladas de mi pasaporte. Hambriento de papel para dibujar

autorretrato con mujer
(como el Marqués de Sade).

Nuevas.
Barcelona.
27. aBril 81.

Testing papers. 10

Barcelona, 27th April 1981

I used up all the free pages left. This, as may be imagined, led to enormous problems and I had the greatest trouble getting myself another passport.

Self-portrait with woman

39

Testing papers. 11

Barcelona, 27th April 1981

Though I am neither a drinker nor addicted to any
kind of drug, people who suffer from those vices
deserve, and get, my fullest understanding.

For I, like them, am a slave to a necessity that admits
no putting off. The need for paper.

I have known many women and been loved by them.
My

Self-portrait with woman (as Bellmer)

Probando
papel
#11

Sin ser yo bebedor ni
adicto a ninguna
clase de drogas, los
que padecen
esos vicios merecen
toda mi comprensión.
Porque yo como ellos
estoy atado a una
necesidad que no
admite prórrogas.
La necesidad
del papel.
He conoci-
do muchas
mujeres
y he sido

amado por
ellas. Mis

[...]
Barcelona
27. IV. 1981.

Autorretrato
con mujer.
(como Bellmer)

41

Testing papers. 12

Barcelona, 27th April 1981

hands have travelled voluptuously over a great variety
of women's skins. I know how to touch them and,
with that touch, produce the ecstasy of love. But no
woman's skin has ever bound me as much as a sheet
of paper.

Self-portrait with woman (as Cézanne)

probando papeles
12.

manos han recorrido
voluptuosamente una gran variedad de
pieles femeninas.
Se tocarlas y producir por
el tacto el
éxtasis amo-
roso. Pero
ninguna
piel femeni-
na me ha
atado
como una
hoja
de
papel.

autoretrato
con mujer
(como Cezanne).

jueves
Barcelona,
27. IV. 1981.

Testing papers. 13

Barcelona, 27th April 1981

The discovery of a new paper, one never used before,
is like an apotheosis. With what intense excitement
one takes one's instrument — pencil, pen or
paintbrush — and travels over that flat plain never
previously explored! It is an excitement I can only
compare to what an explorer feels when he finally
gets to the top of a mountain he has set himself as a
goal.

On these sheets of different sorts of paper, which a
friend who knows my cravings has been good enough
to give me, I have gradually done some drawings and
written some lines which are intended as a homage to
the character to whom I owe so much: paper.

Self-portrait with model

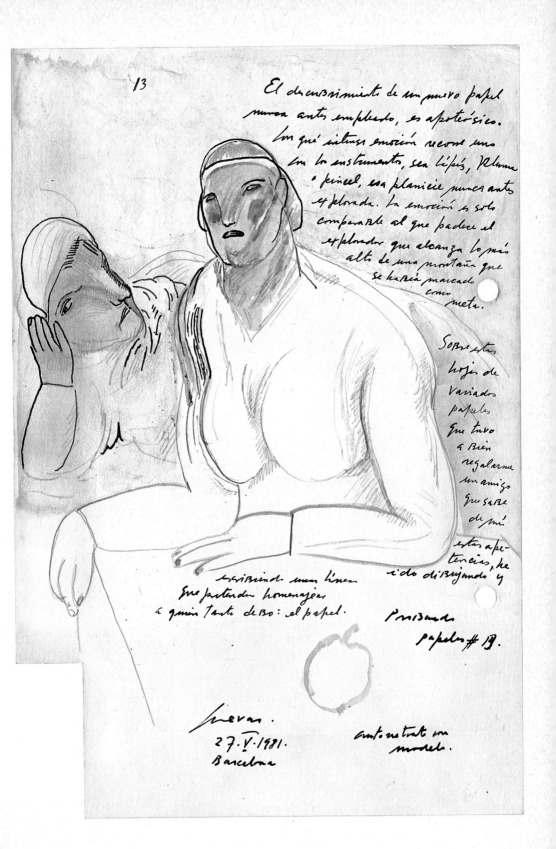

Testing papers. 14

Barcelona, 27th April 1981

A sheet of drawing paper can be magnificent or
wretched. Its fate is determined by the artist who
carries it off to his studio. How sorry I feel for all
those splendid sheets sullied by coarse, mediocre
artists.

Those sheets will be condemned to bear for ever a
feeble, wretched image. It would be better for them if
some compassionate soul were to destroy them by
throwing them into the fire.

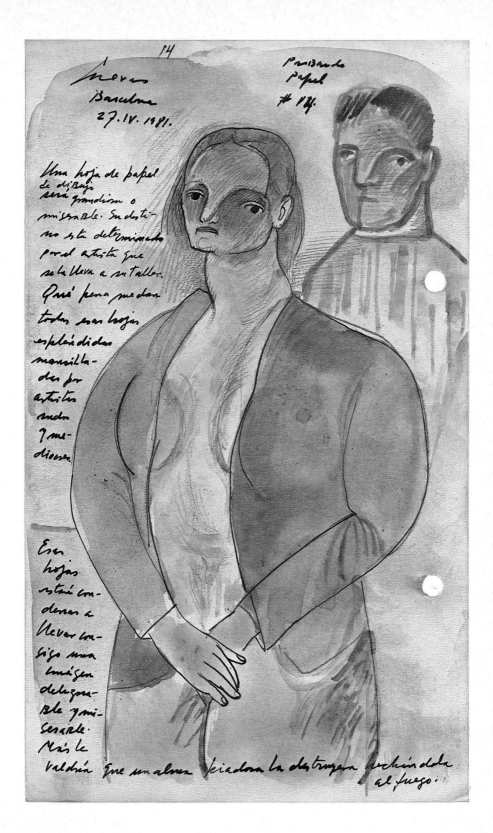

14

Nieves
Barcelona
27.IV.1981.

Probando
Papel
14.

Una hoja de papel
de dibujo
será grandiosa o
miserable. Su desti-
no esta determinado
por el artista que
se la lleva a su taller.

Qué pena me dan
todas esas hojas
espléndidas
mancilla-
das por
artistas
rudos
y me-
diocres.

Esas
hojas
están con-
denas a
llevar con-
sigo una
imágen
desagra-
ble y mi-
serable.
Más le
valdría que un alma piadosa la destruyera hechándola
al fuego.

47

Testing papers. 15

Barcelona, 27th April 1981

But do you realize what happens when a sheet of
paper falls into the hands of a Picasso, or into those
of a Matisse or an Ingres? That sheet is transformed
into a marvellous world of stains and lines. As time
goes by it will grow old and get stained, but there will
always be skillful restorers to look after it and protect
it from the light.

Those privileged sheets of paper will contain for ever
a moment of the inspiration of the great creators —
those great creators who are gods remaking the world
every day.

Self-portrait with woman

15

¿Pero os dais cuenta de lo que sucede cuando una hoja cae en manos de un Picasso o de un Matisse o de un Ingres? Esa hoja se convierte en un mundo maravilloso de manchas y líneas. Con el tiempo envejecerá y se manchará, pero siempre tendrá a su disposición a sabios restauradores que la cuidarán y la protegerán de la luz.

Esas hojas de papel privilegiadas contendrán para siempre un momento de inspiración de los grandes creadores que son dioses que hacen el mundo todos los días.

autorretrato con mujer.

Saura.
27·IV·81.
Barcelona.

Probando papel # 15

Testing papers. 16

Barcelona, 27th April 1981

What is it that leads an artist to prefer one particular paper to another? The paper that Ingres preferred

Self-portrait with models

Probando
papel
16.

¿Que lleva a los artistas
a preferir un papel por encima
de otro? El papel que pre-
fería
Ingres

entimistat
los modelos.

Cuevas
Barcelona
27. IV. 81.

Testing papers. 17

Barcelona, 27th April 1981

is not the same one that found favor with Daumier or
Toulouse-Lautrec. There are artists who "make
themselves comfortable" with one sort of paper and
nobody can persuade them to leave that "armchair." I,
however, feel equally at ease with all kinds. I am not
faithful to any one paper.

Self-portrait with old woman

53

Testing papers. 18

Barcelona, 27th April 1981

In this matter of papers I am both fickle and
frivolous. Quite scatterbrained. I do one drawing on a
smooth surface, and then for my next I am looking for
its opposite: a paper with a pronounced grain. While I
am fond of Italian papers, I am also fascinated by the
ones made in Germany or in France and, of course, by
Japanese papers.

Even with those poor Manila papers, or with the sort
used for wrapping bread in or for printing newspapers,
I can always manage to do something worthwhile.

Self-portrait with woman

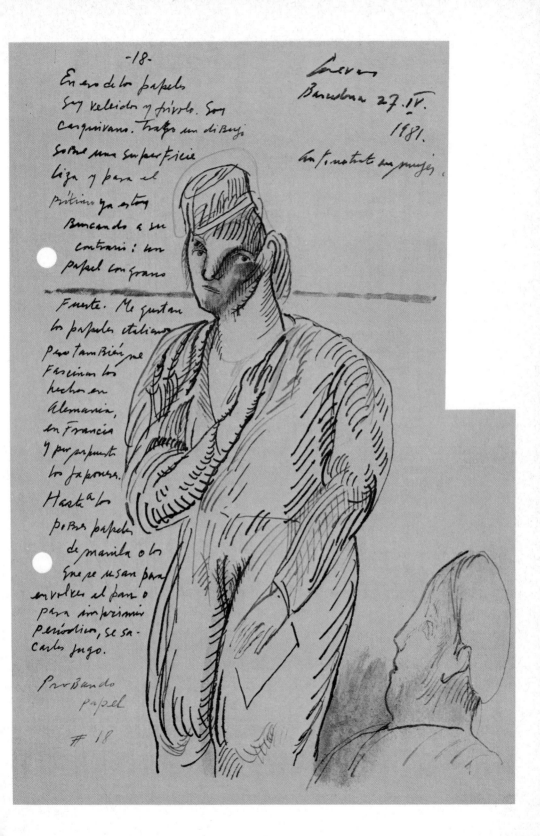

-18-

En eso de los papeles
soy veleidoso y frívolo. Soy
casquivano. Trazo un dibujo
sobre una superficie
lisa y para el
próximo ya estoy
    Buscando a su
    contrario: un
    papel con grano

fuerte. Me gustan
los papeles italianos
pero también me
fascinan los
hechos en
Alemania,
en Francia
y por supuesto
los japoneses.
Hasta los
    pobres papeles
    de manila o los
    que se usan para
envolver el pan o
para imprimir
periódicos, se sa-
carles jugo.

Probando
    papel

18

Caevers
Barcelona 27. IV.
            1981.
...

Testing papers. 19

Barcelona, 27th April 1981

There are papers which have been made for
watercolor, others for pastel, crayon or pencil. Others
again are prepared for silverpoint. I use them in the
most anarchic way possible.

The ones that are said to be intended only for pastel,
I wet with great brushstrokes of gouache. And the
ones suitable for watercolor I use for charcoal
drawings. It is interesting to tame papers. They are all
noble materials if you know how to treat them.

Self-portrait with woman

—

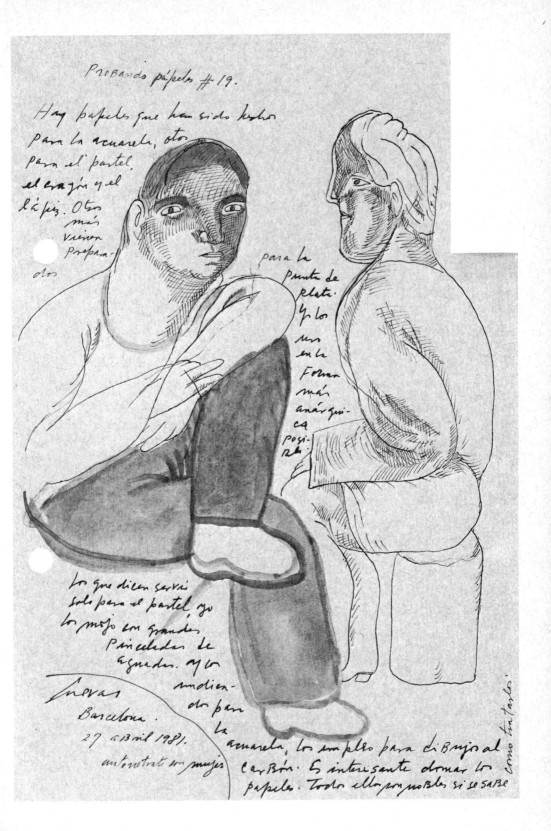

Probando papeles #19.

Hay papeles que han sido hechos para la acuarela, otros para el pastel, el crayón y el lápiz. Otros más fueron preparados

para la punta de plata. Y los más en la forma más anárquica posible.

Los que dicen servir solo para el pastel, yo los mojo con grandes pinceladas de aguadas. Y los indicados para la acuarela, los empleo para dibujar al carbón. Es interesante domar los papeles. Todos ellos son nobles si se sabe como tratarlos.

Cuevas
Barcelona.
27 abril 1981.
autorretrato con mujer

Testing papers. 20

Barcelona, 27th April 1981

When I am dead my permanence in this world will be decided by all the papers I have covered with my scrawls.

I have been a sort of notary, gradually making up an inventory of all that it has fallen to my lot to see and feel. And for this notarial work of mine I used the humblest material that came to my hand: paper.

My work began thanks to the fortuitous fact of having been born in a factory that made it. I always had

Self-portrait with woman

Probando papel # 20.

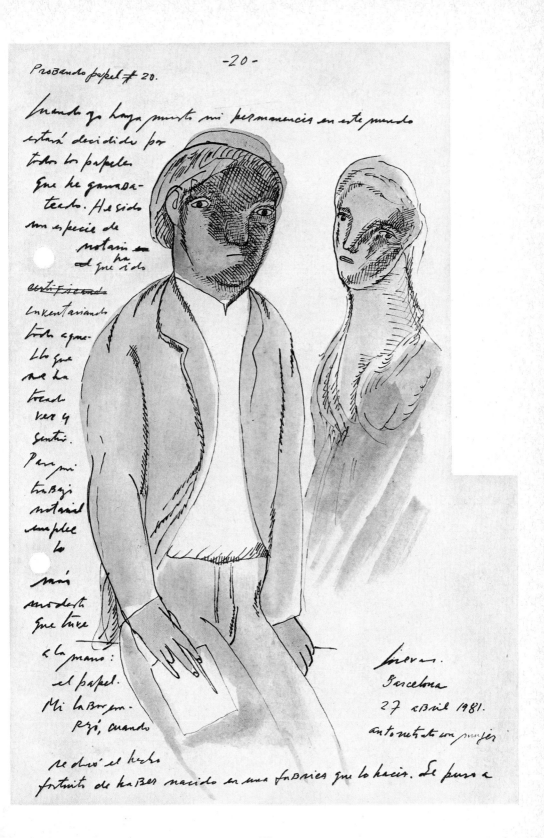

Cuando yo haya muerto mi permanencia en este mundo
estará decidida por
todos los papeles
que he ganada-
teado. Ha sido
una especie de
notario en
el que ha sido
certificando
inventariando
todo aque-
llo que
me ha
tocado
ver y
sentir.
Para mi
trabajo
notarial
empleé
lo
más
modesto
que tuve
a la mano:
el papel.
Mi la Borges.
Pero, cuando

se dio el hecho
fortuito de haber nacido en una fábrica que lo hacía. Se puso a

Brevas.
Barcelona
27 abril 1981.
autorretrato con mujer

59

Testing papers. 21

Barcelona, 27th April 1981

at my disposal all the paper I wanted. Silently, I
hurled myself at an immense sheet that had just been
turned out of a machine and began to take notes.

These papers would be more suitable for pastel.

I also like colored papers. But I prefer to color the
backgrounds for myself.

Self-portrait with woman

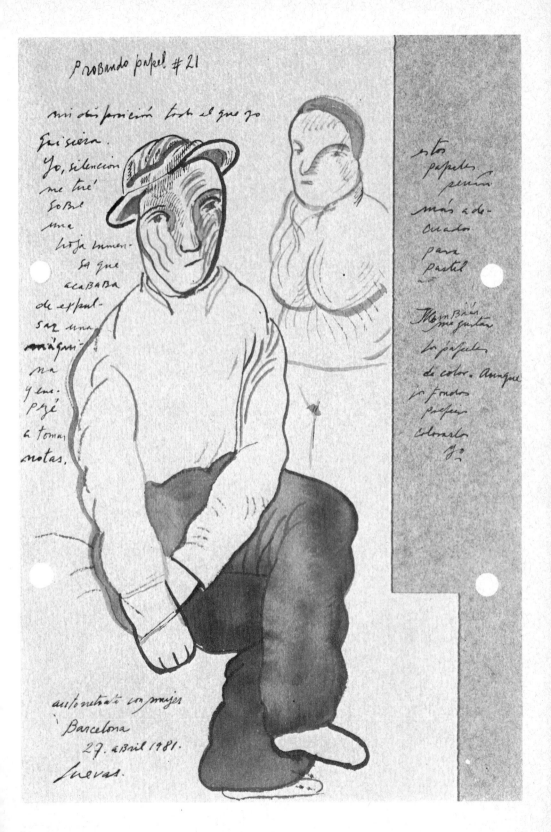

proBando papel #21

mi disposición toda el que yo
quisiera.
Yo, silencio
me tiré
sobre
una
hoja inmen-
sa que
acaBaBa
de expul-
sar una
máquina
y me.
pusé
a tomar
notas.

estos
papeles
serán
más a de-
cuado
para
pastel

También
me gustan
los papeles
de color. Aunque
fondos
prefiero
colorarlos
yo.

autorretrato con mujer
Barcelona
27. aBril 1981.
Cuevas.

61

Testing papers. 22

Barcelona, 27th April 1981

Well, dear Juan. I have ranged too far. The attraction of these little papers has brought me to the excess of this letter.

I'll see you in Parets del Vallès. I think the engravings are going well. Anyway, you'll have a look at them.

With my most cordial good wishes:

José Luis Cuevas

My best regards to Eugenia and the lovely Patricia.

Probando papel # 22.

Bueno querido Juan,
Ya me extendí dema-
siado. La seducción
de estos papelitos me
llevaron al exceso de
esta carta.
Nos veremos en
Parets de Vallès. Creo
que los grabados van
Bien. Ya les ~~harás~~
hecharás un ojo.
Te saluda frater-
nalmente:
José Luis
Cuevas

Muchos saludos para Eugenia
y la Bella Patricia.

Barcelona
27 abril
1981.

DRAWINGS
Testing papers Nos. 1 to 74

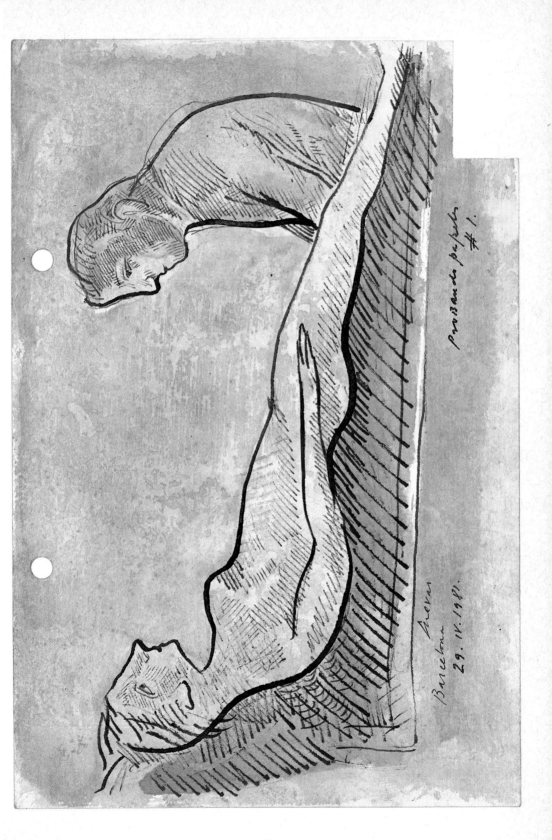

Savova Barcelona 29.IV.1981.

probando papeles #2.

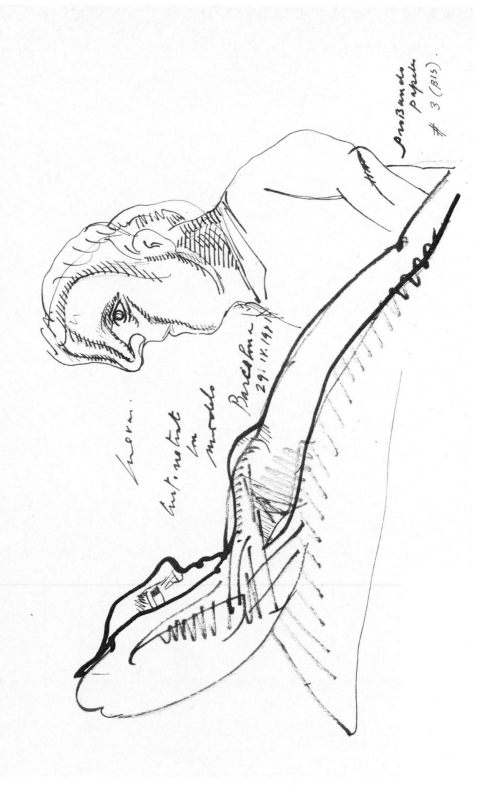

Nova
Barcelona
29.IV.1981.

Probando papeles
#4.

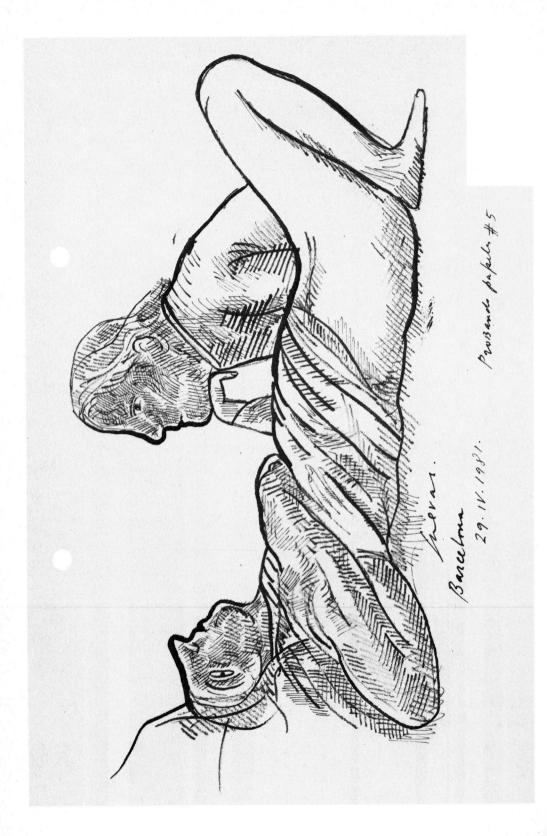

Prova.

Barcelona

29.IV.1981.

Paisano papila #5

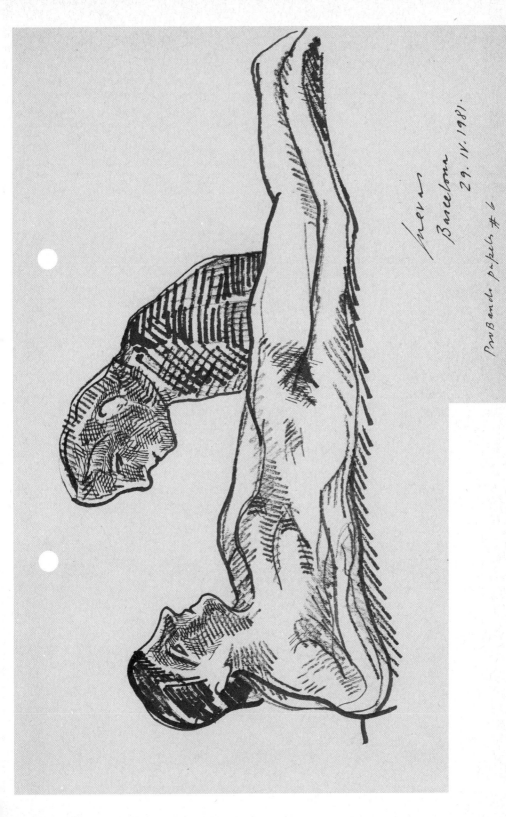

PmiBando papels # 6

Barcelona
29. IV. 1981.

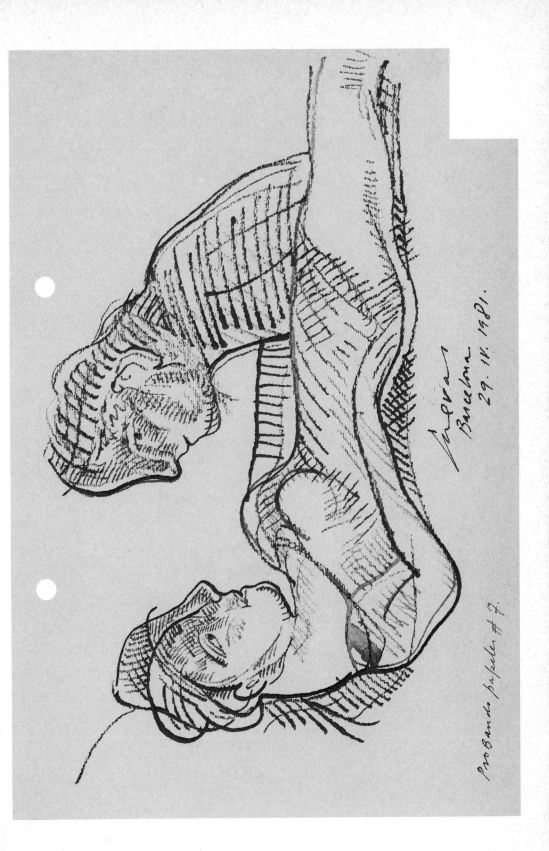

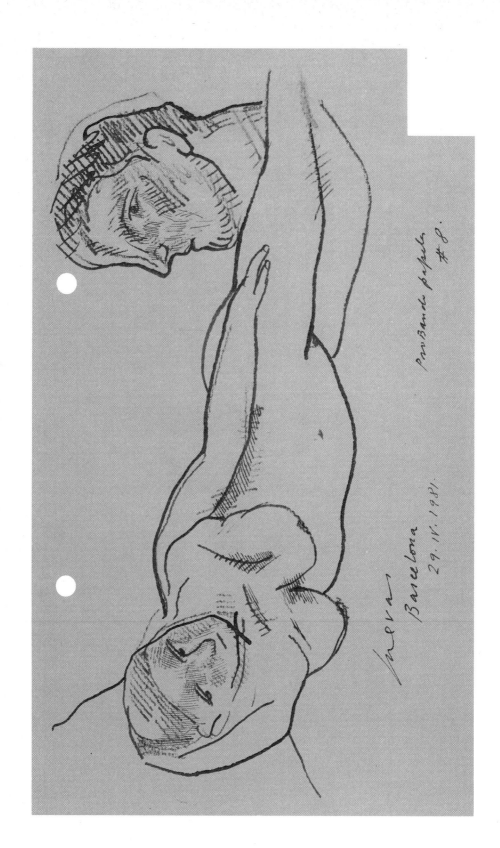

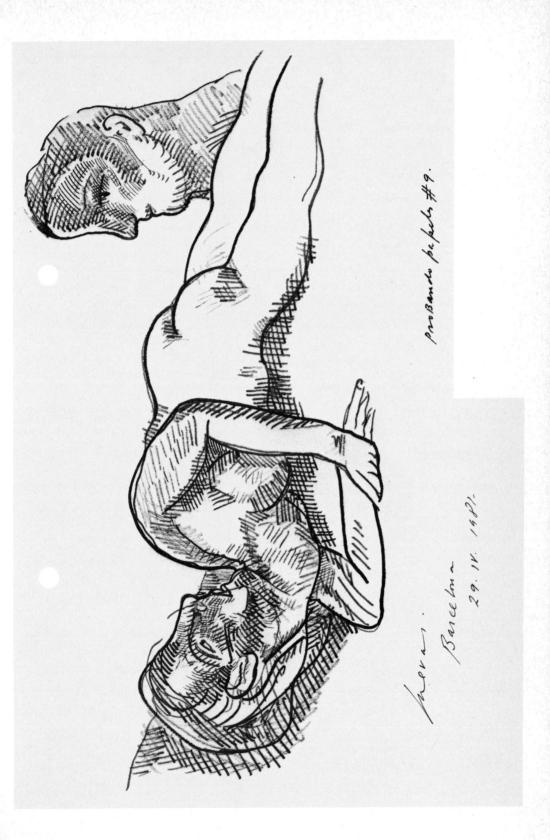

Probando papeles #9.

Nieva.
Barcelona
29.IV. 1981.

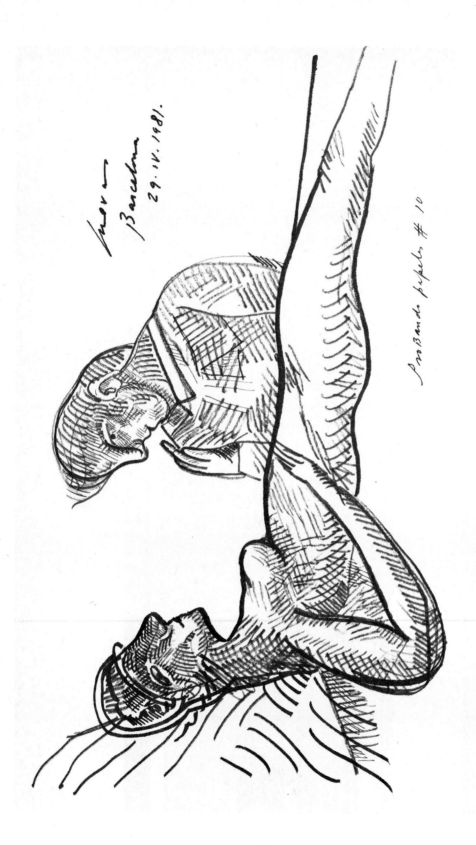

Barcelona
29.IV.1981.

Probando papeles # 10

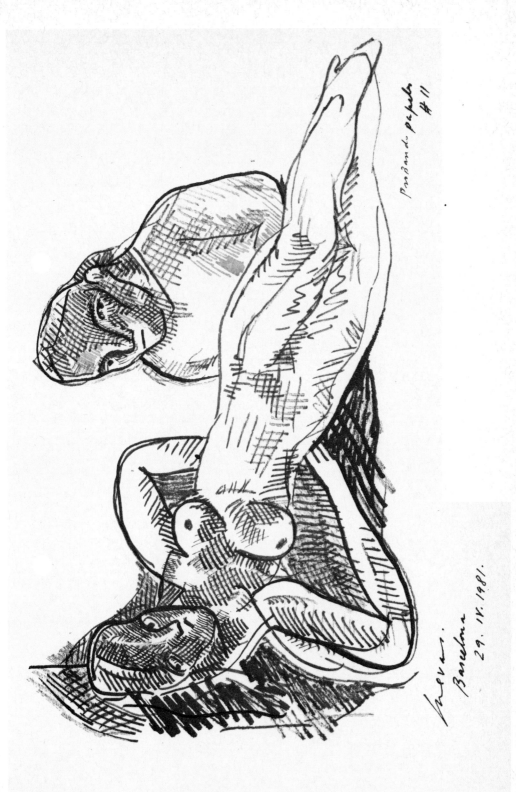

Probando papeles #11

Barcelona
29. IV. 1981.

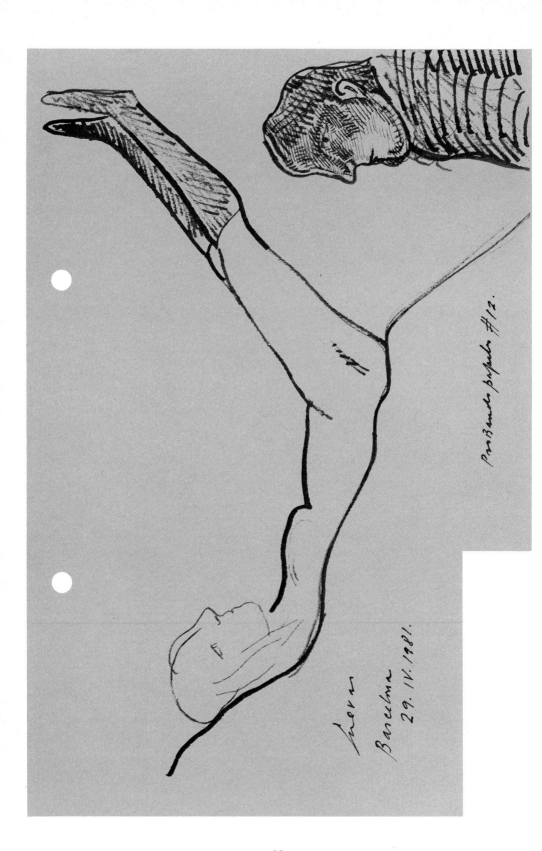

Barcelona
29. IV. 1981.

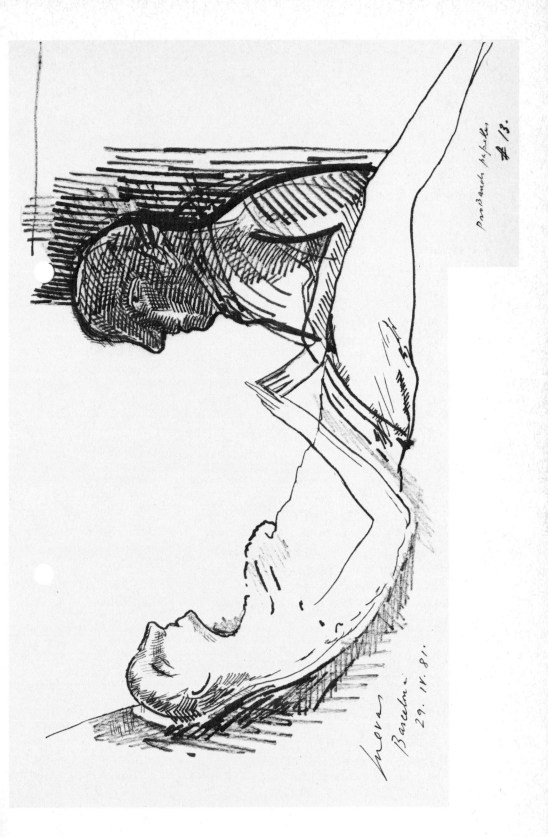

Pruebas de papeles # 14.

Barcelona
29. IV. 1981.

Nevas Barcelona. 29. IV. 1981.

por Benito

papeles # 15

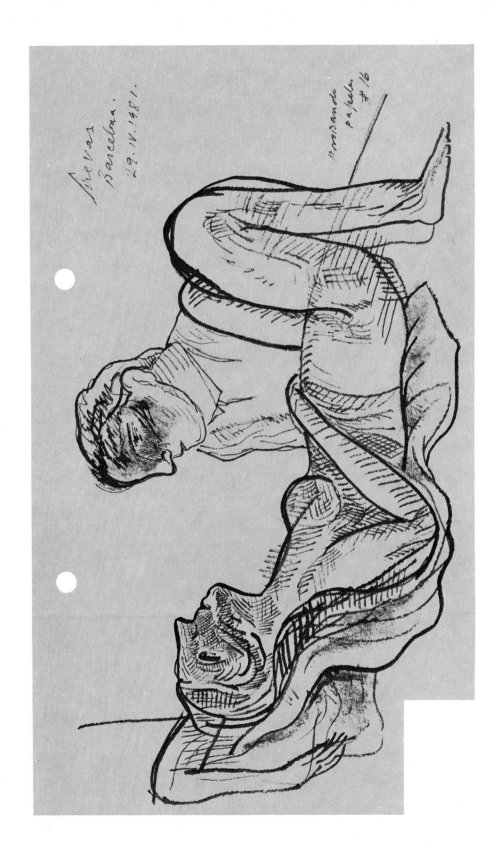

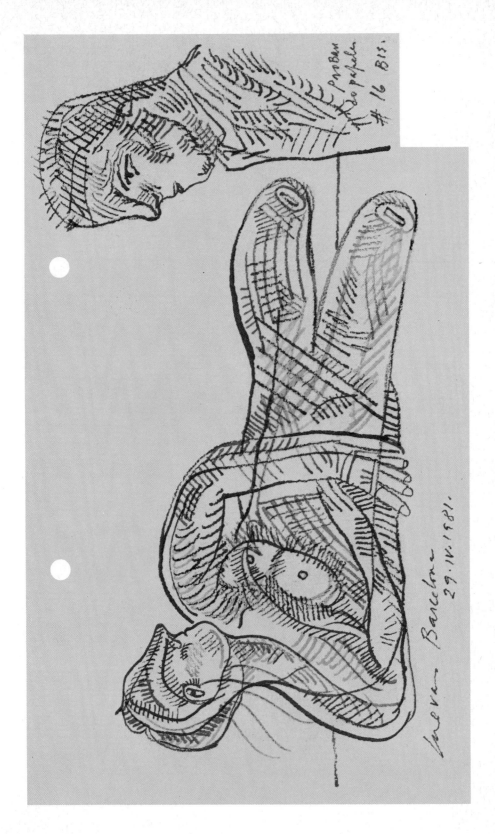

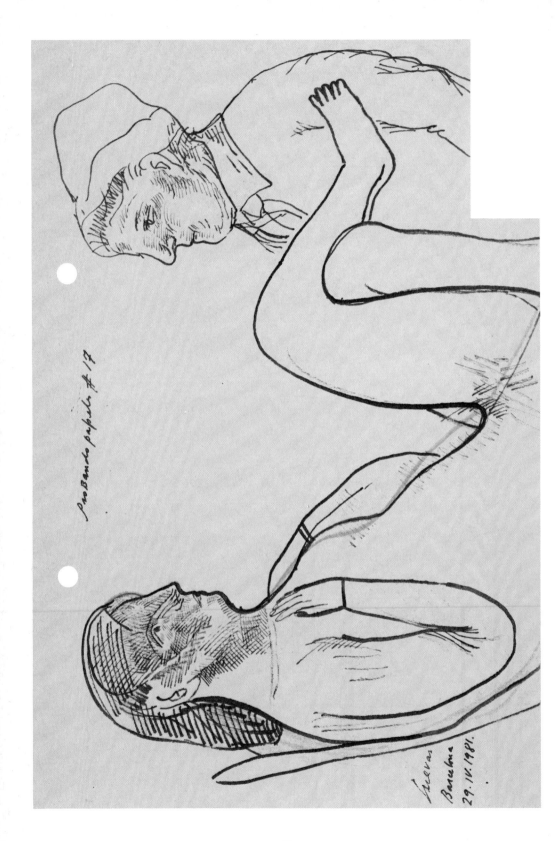

San Bando proposta # 17

Steva
Barcelona
29. IV. 1981.

86

Presidente populi #18

Guevara
Barcelona
29.IV.1981.

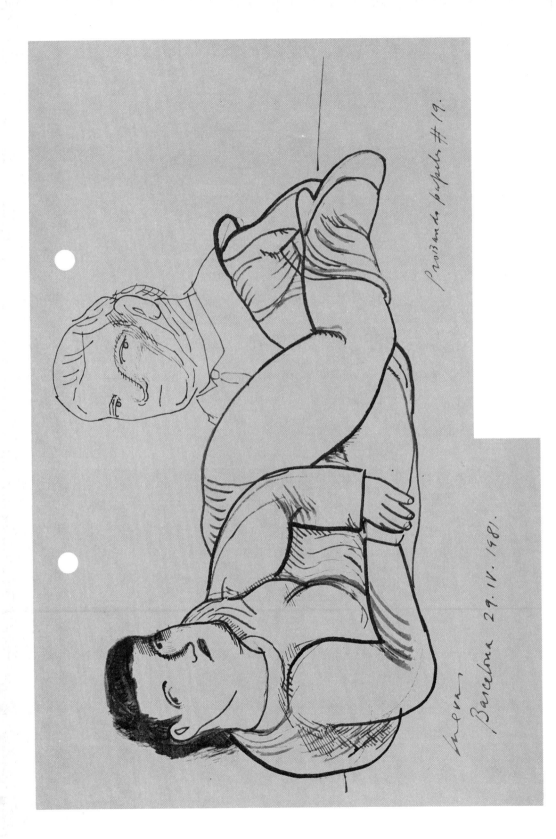

Presents Picasso #19.

Sacra,

Barcelona 29. IV. 1981.

88

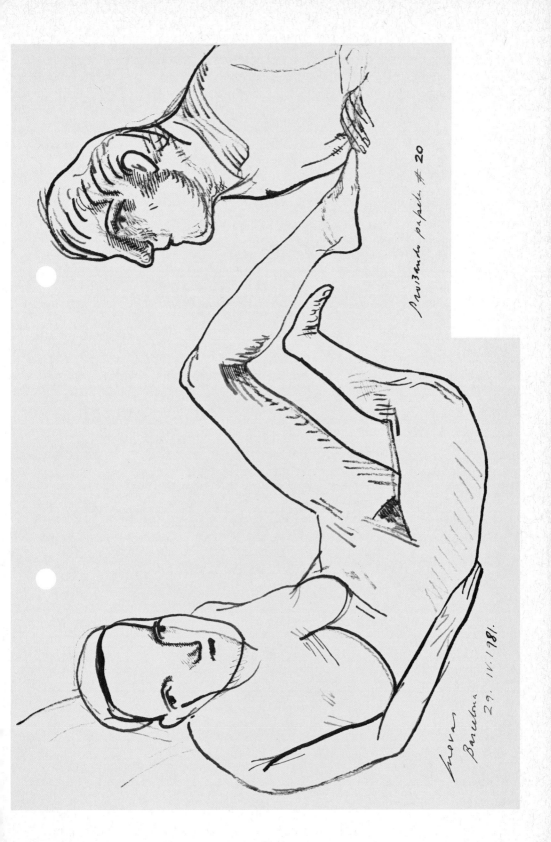

Dibuixants papers. # 20

Guinovart
Barcelona
29. IV. 1981.

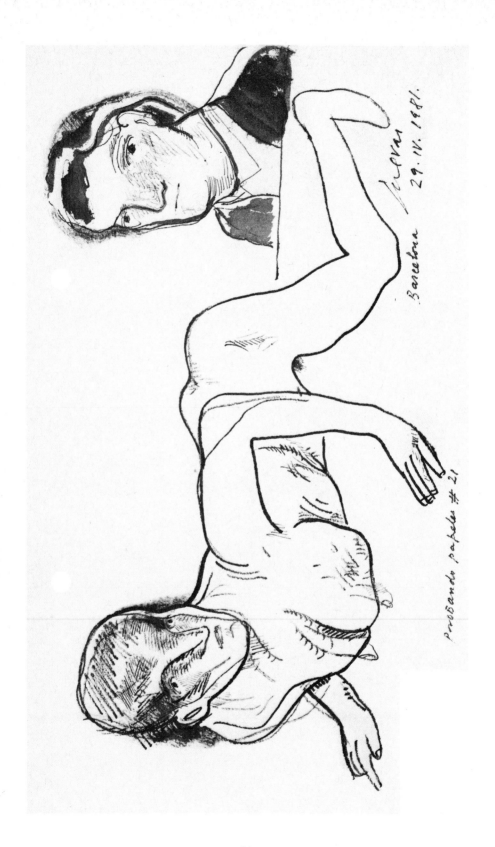

Barcelona — 29. IV. 1981.

Probando papeles # 21

90

Fred van
Baarsen

29.IV.1981.

ProBando pr fecha # 22.

Nueva
Barcelona
29. IV. 81.

Pastel en papel # 23.

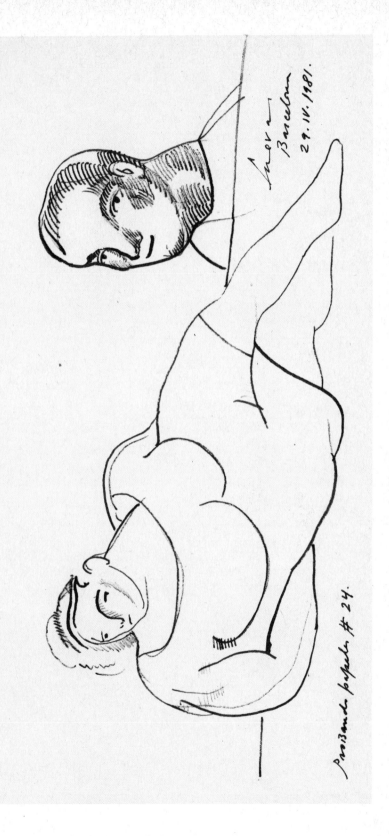

Sueva
Barcelona
29.IV.1981.

Praizanda Isquela # 24.

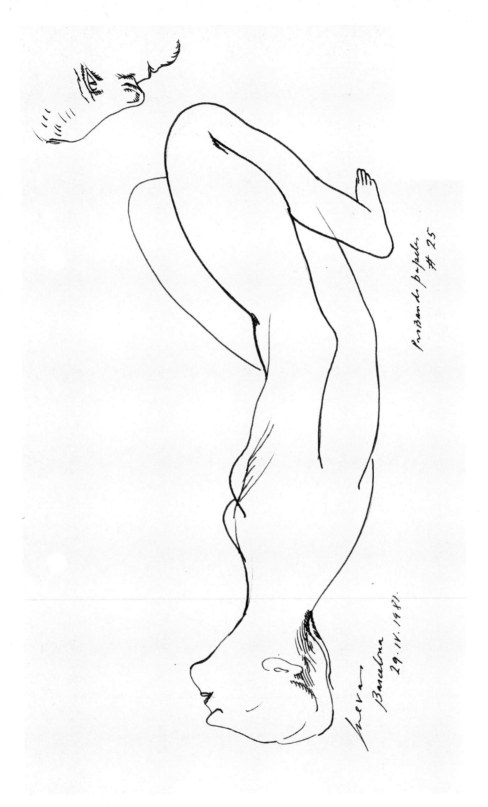

Profundo profiles # 25

Nova
Barcelona
29.IV.1981.

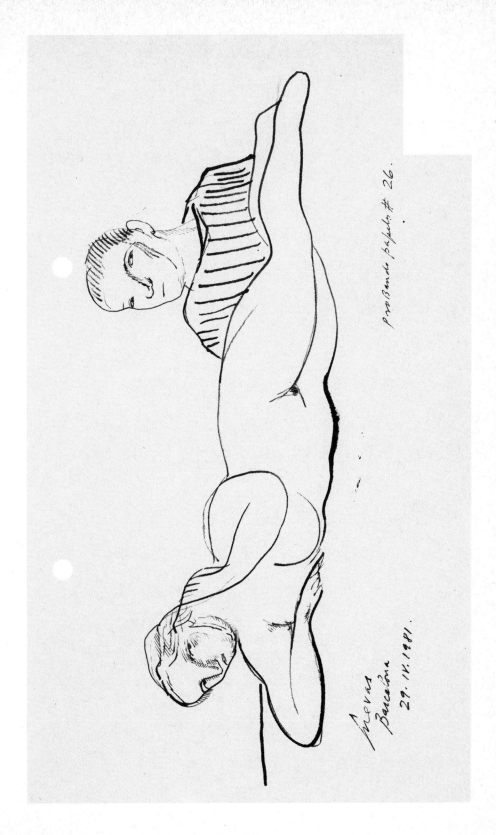

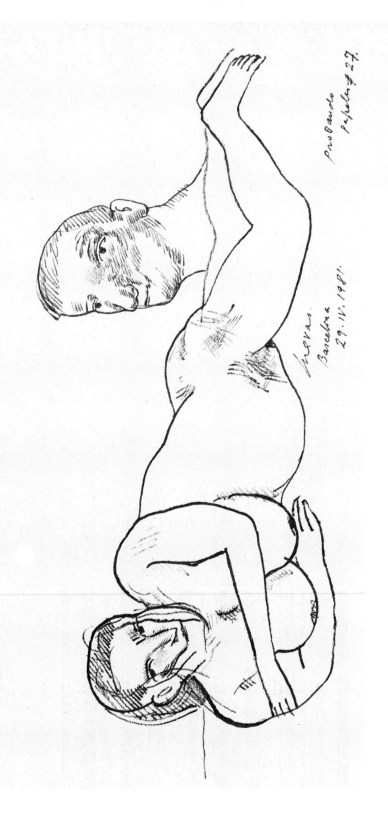

Cuevas.
Barcelona
29.IV.1981.

Probando
Pastales #27.

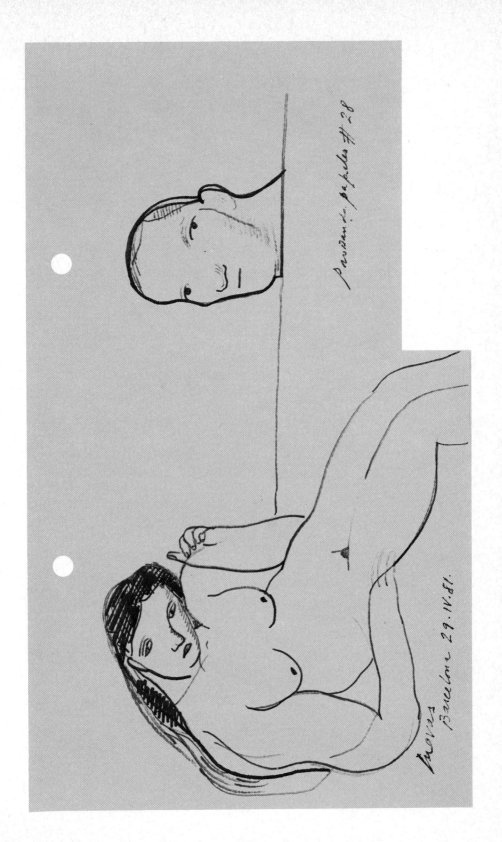

Pinturas papeles # 28

Nieves Barcelona 29.IV.81.

97

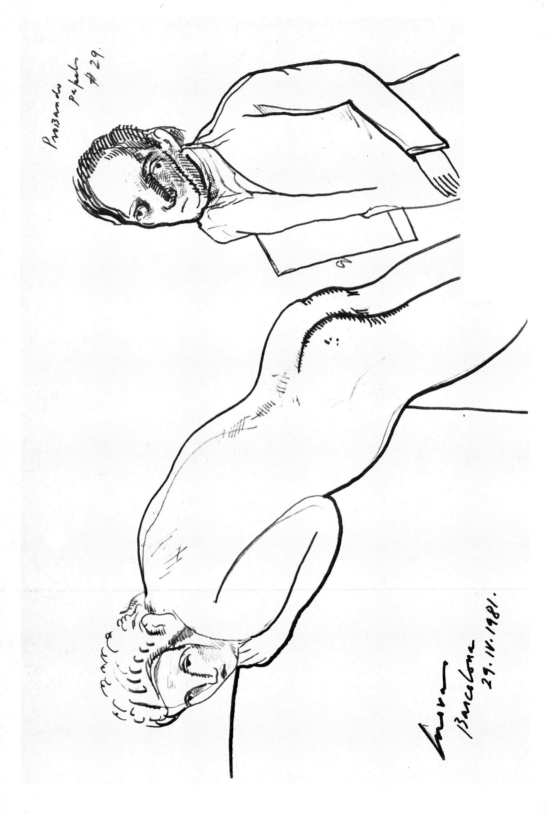

Pensando Papeles # 29.

Barcelona
27.IV.1981.

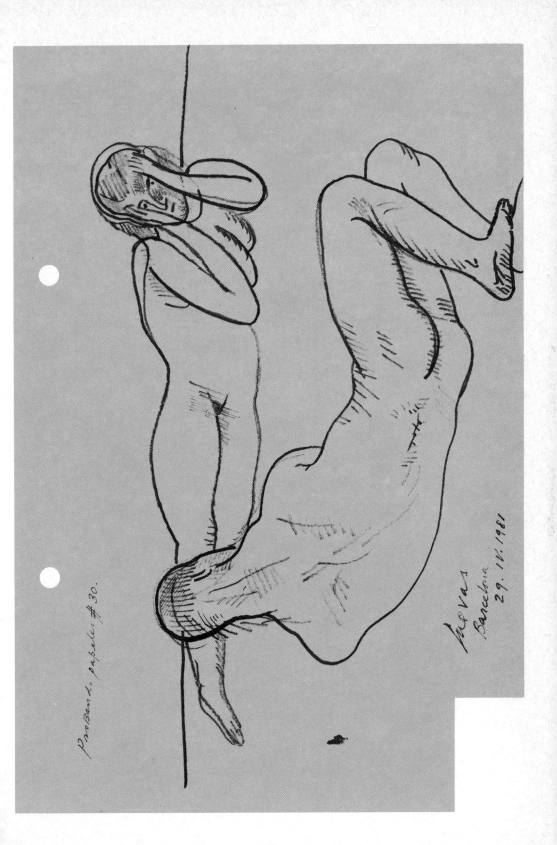

Probando papeles # 30.

Vargas
Barcelona
29. IV. 1981

99

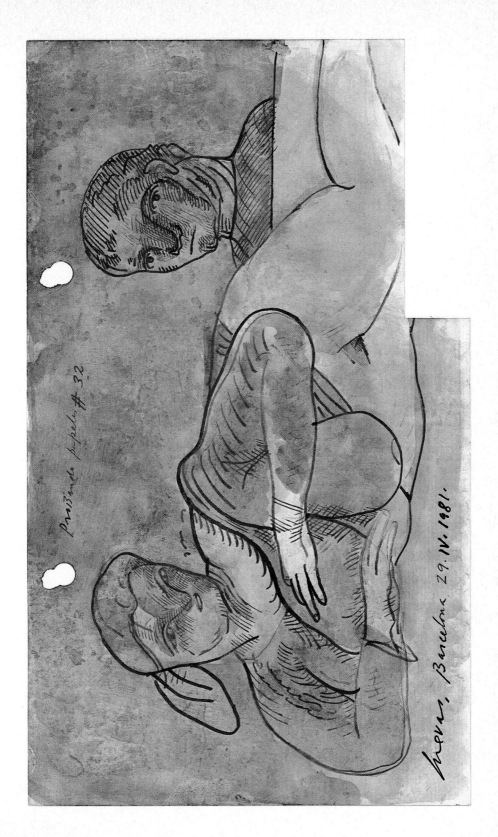

Retrato inédito # 32

Arenas, Barcelona, 29. IV. 1981.

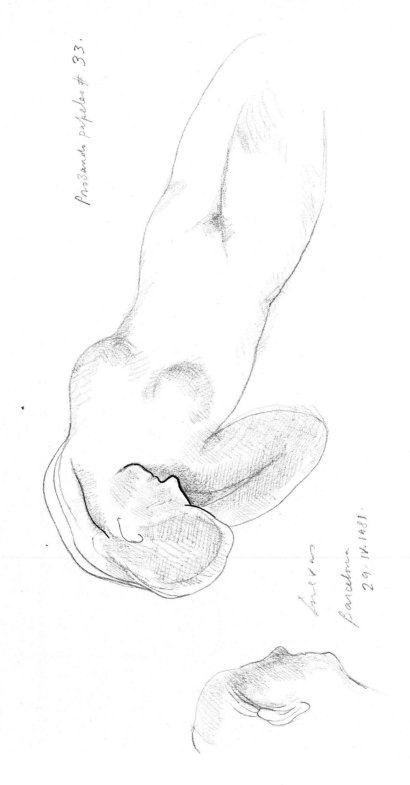

Probando papeles # 33.

Suévas
Barcelona
29.IV.1983.

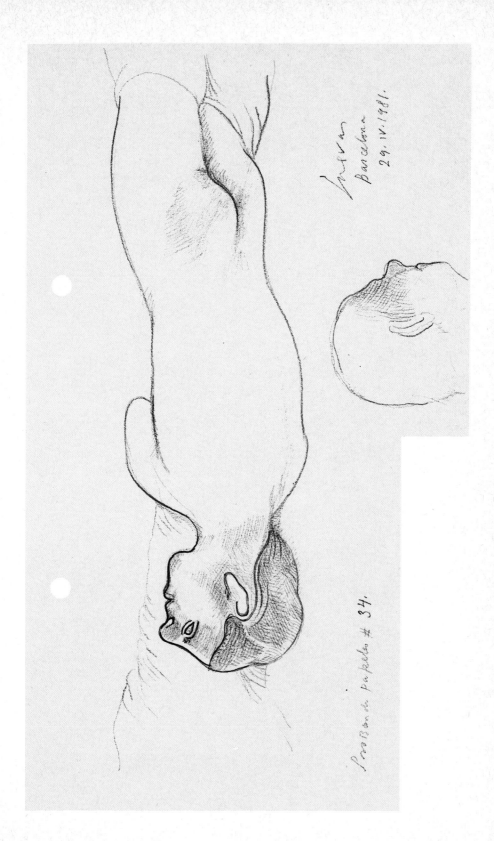

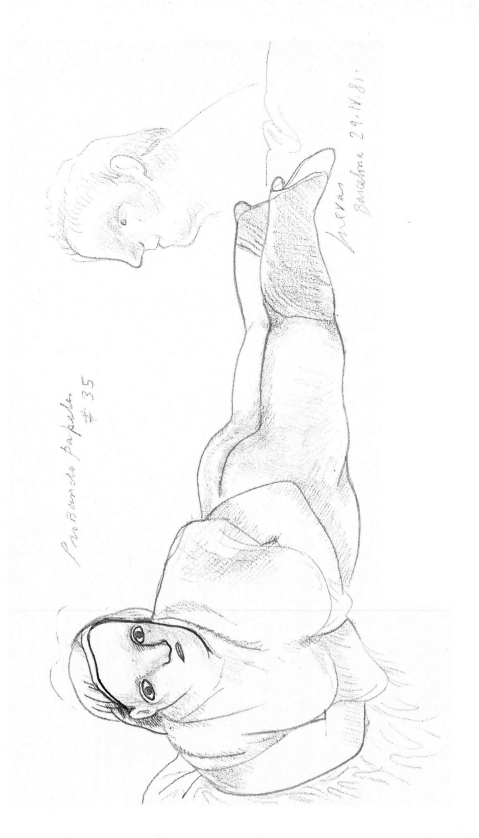

Cuevas

Probando papel. # 36

Barcelona 29. IV. 1981.

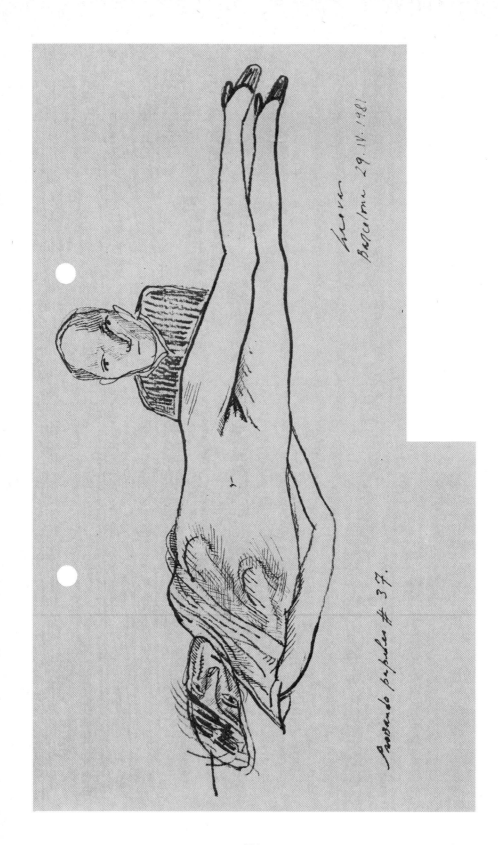

106

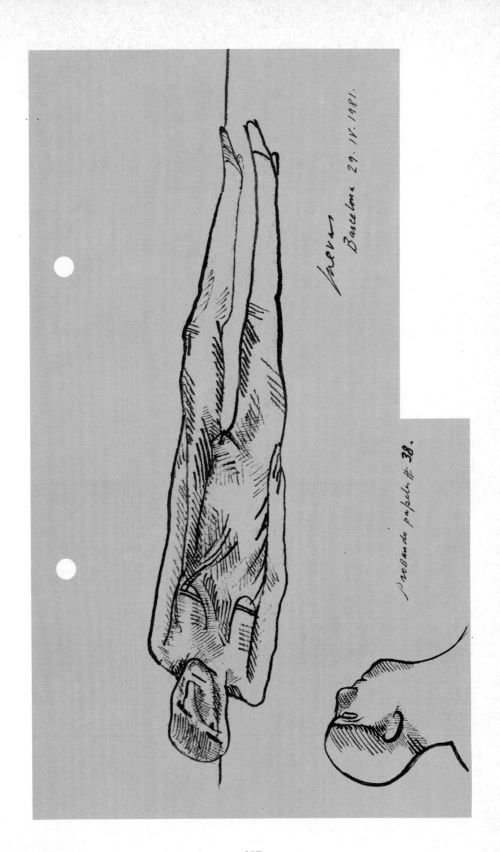

Barcelona 29. IV. 1981.

107

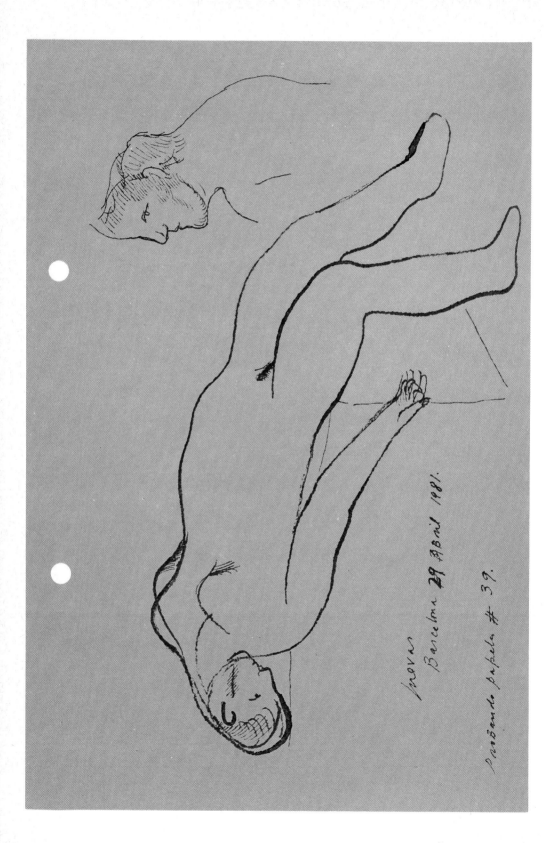

Inova
Barcelona 29 Abril 1981.

Pasando papeles # 39.

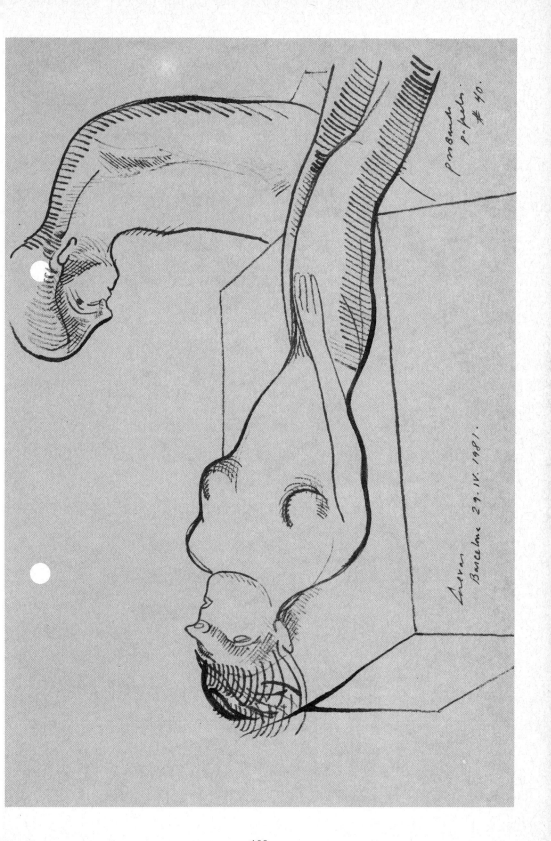

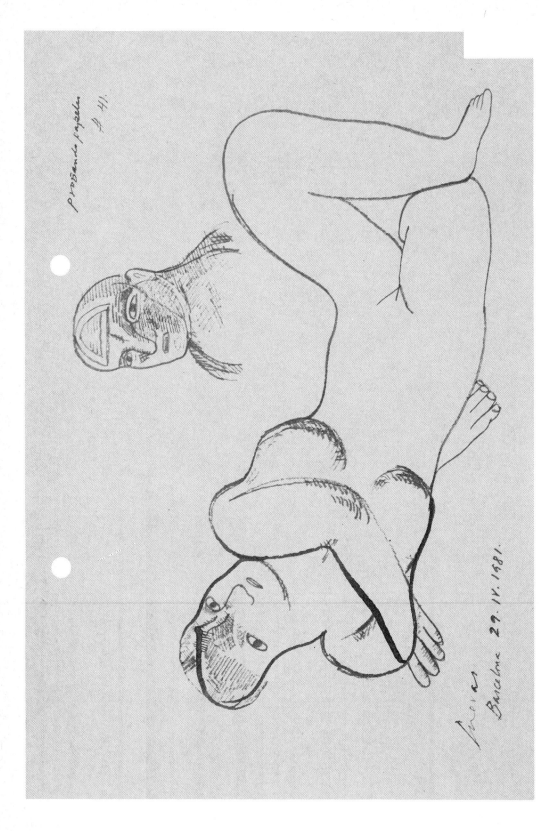

Barcelona 29.IV.1981.

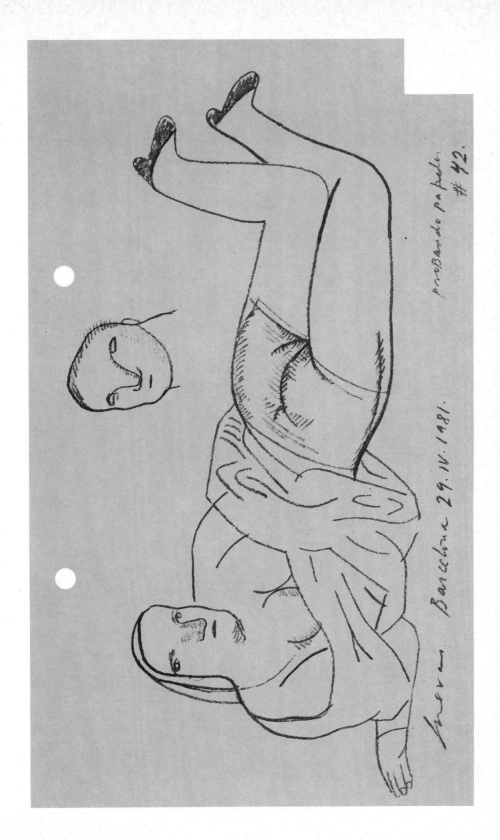

Barcelona 29.IV.1981.

probando papeles. # 42.

Probando
papeles
43

Cuevas Barcelona 29. IV. 1981.

113

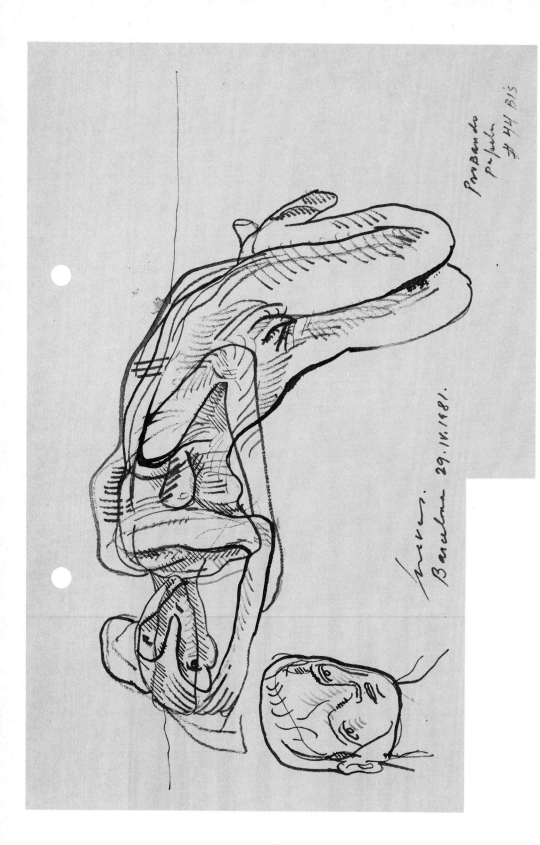

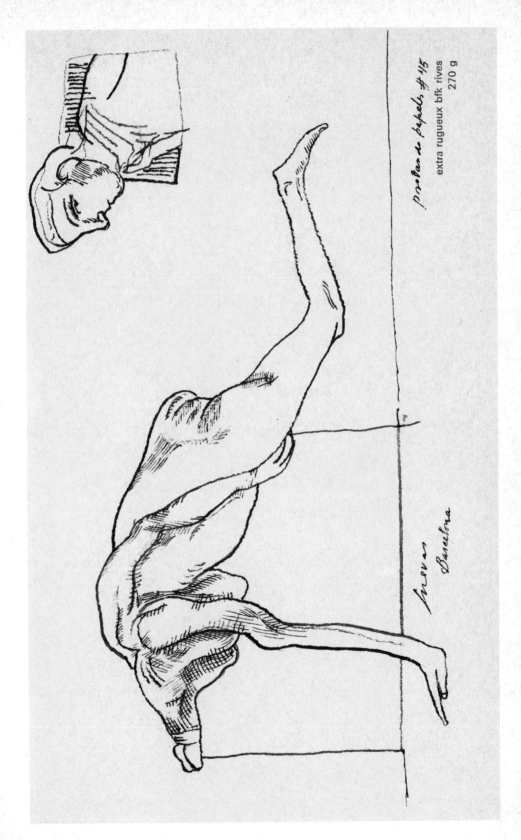

protem de papels #45
extra rugueux bfk rives
270 g

Breitband
Papela # 46
vélin arches blanc
160 g

Barcelona 29. IV. 1981.

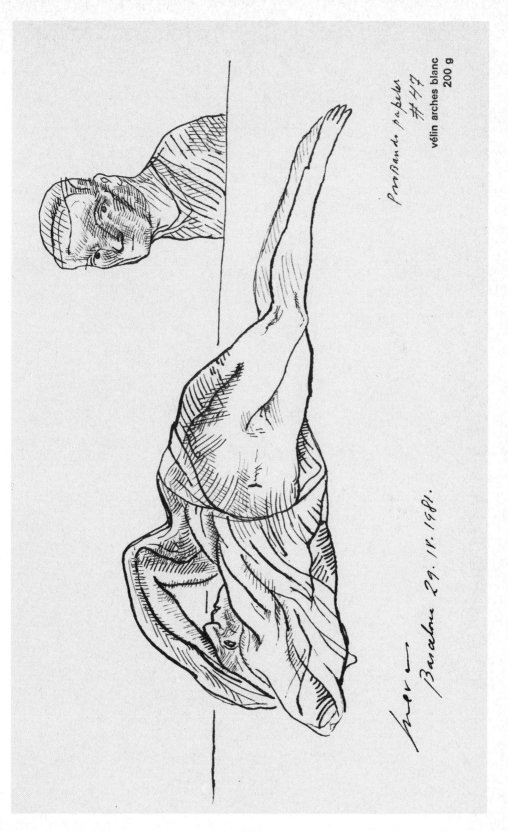

profonde papéer
#47
vélin arches blanc
200 g

Barcelone 29. IV. 1981.

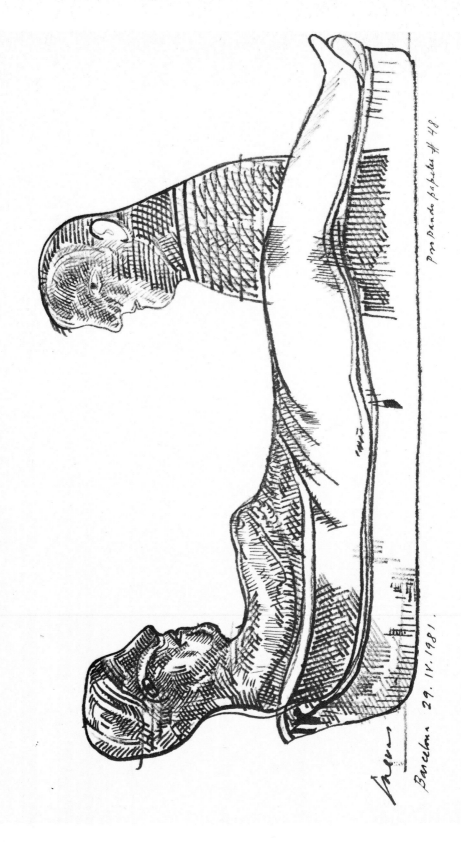

Propaganda Pipher #48.

Barcelona 29. IV. 1981.

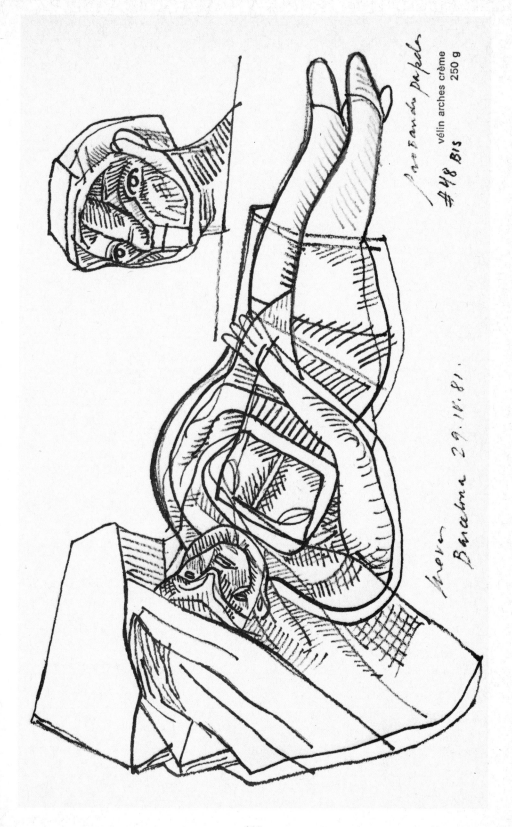

sur franche papeln
vélin arches crème
250 g
#48 BIS

Snow
Barcelona 29.10.81.

119

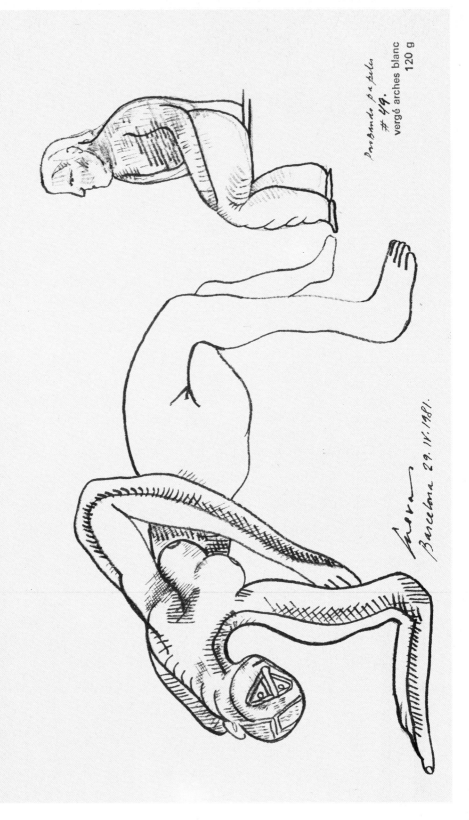

Drawing paper
#49.
vergé arches blanc
120 g

Barcelona 29.IV.1981.

Prueba
papeta # 50
japon nacré
180 g

Grova
Barcelona 29. IV. 1981.

121

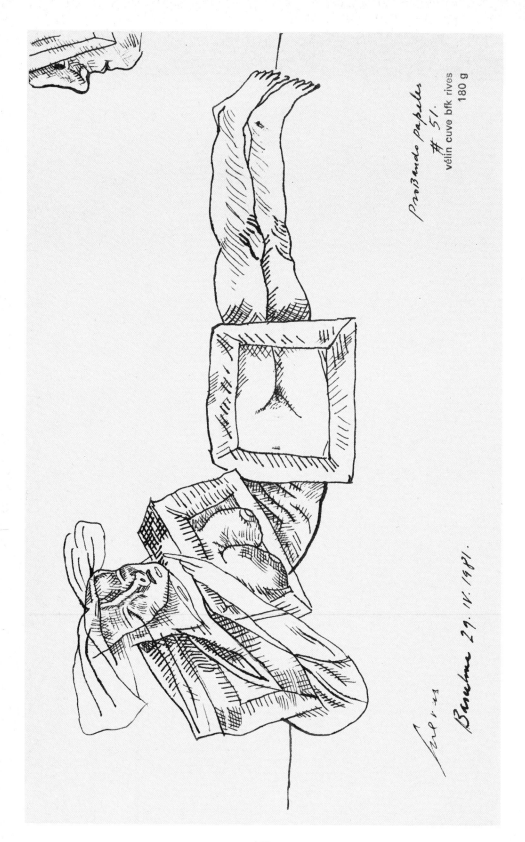

Probando papeles
51.
vélin cuve bfk rives
180 g

Barcelona 27. IV. 1981.

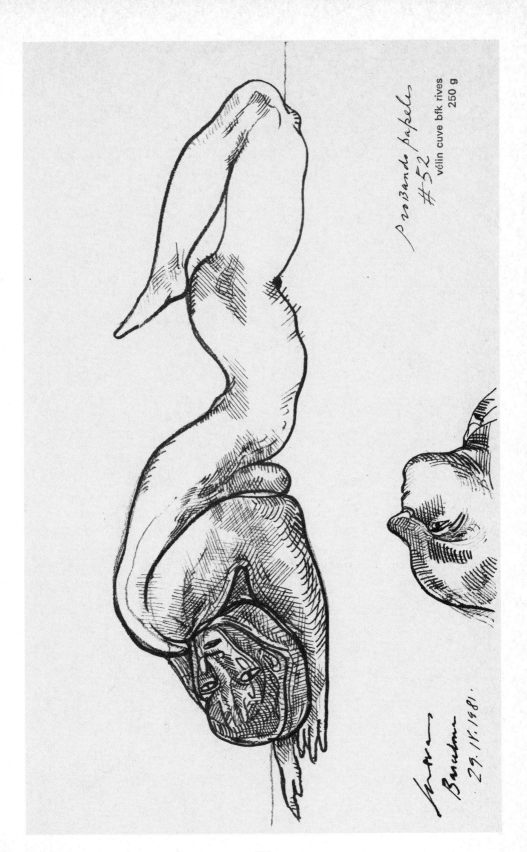

Probando papeles
#52
vélin cuve bfk rives
250 g

29.IV.1981.

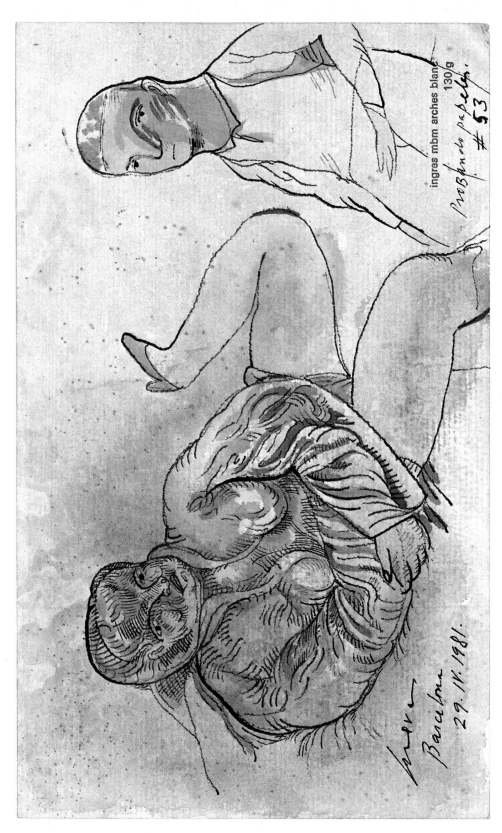

ingras mbm arches blanc
130/g

Probhedo papelar.
53

Barcelma
29.IV.1981.

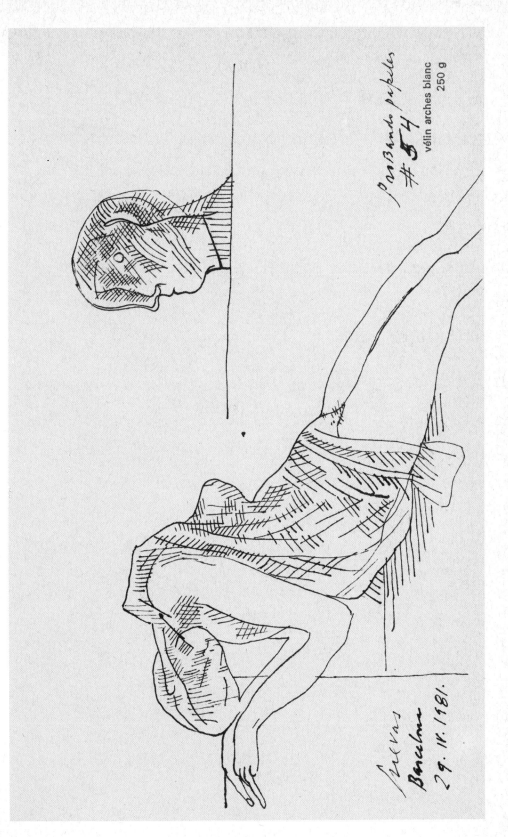

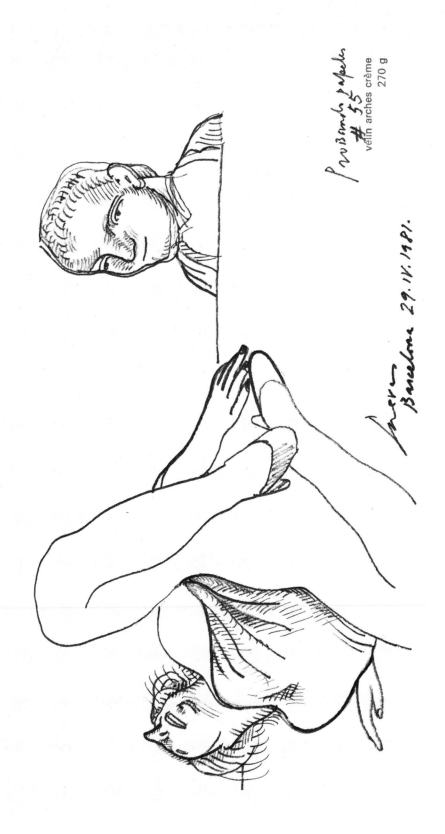

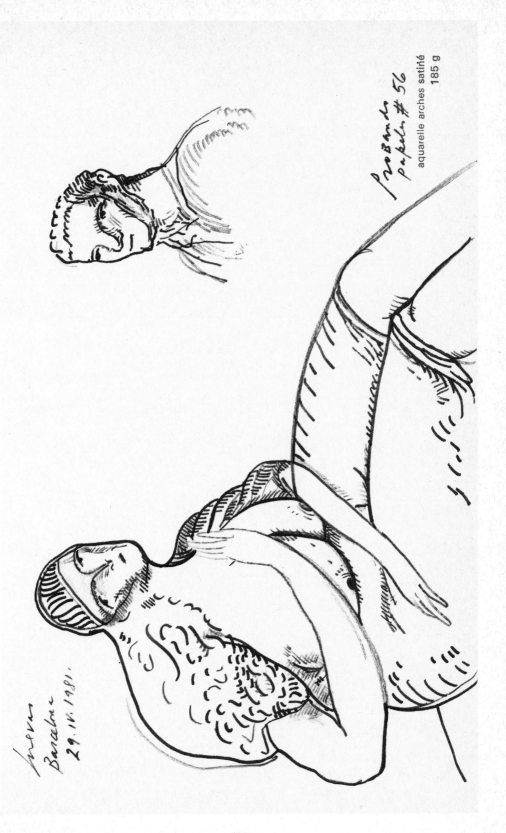

Barcelone
29.IV.1981.

Brassens
papier # 56
aquarelle arches satiné
185 g

Probando
papeles

57.

Barcelona
29. IV. 1981.

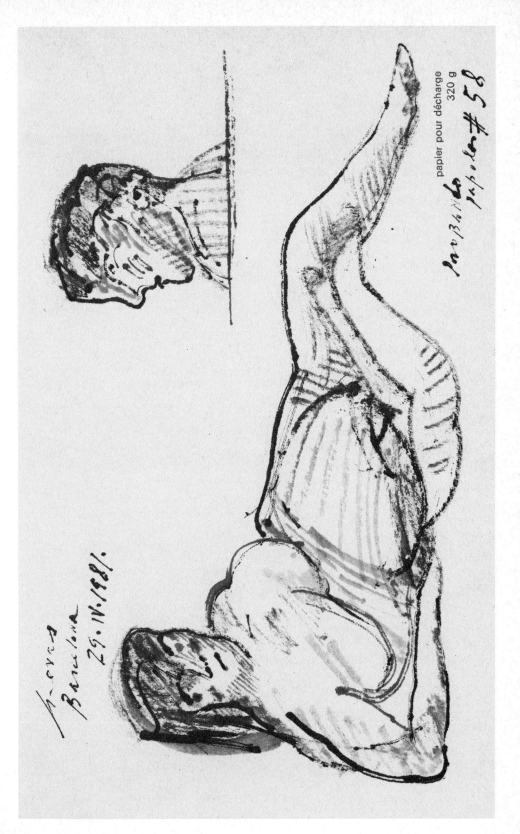

papier pour décharge
320 g

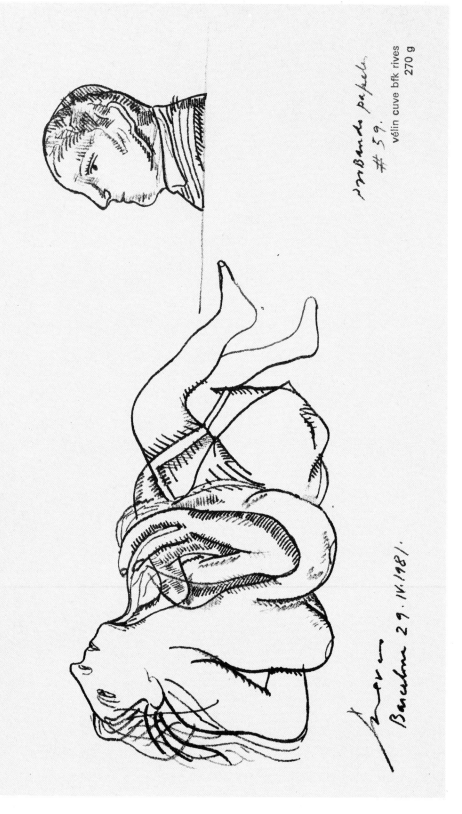

Pruebas de papel
#59.
vélin cuve bfk rives
270 g

Barcelona 27.IV.1981.

Probando papeles # 61.

Barcelona 29.IV.1981.

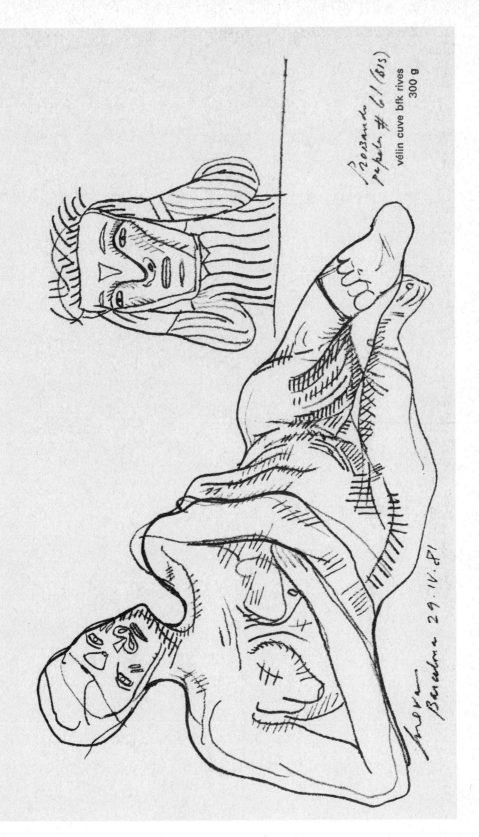

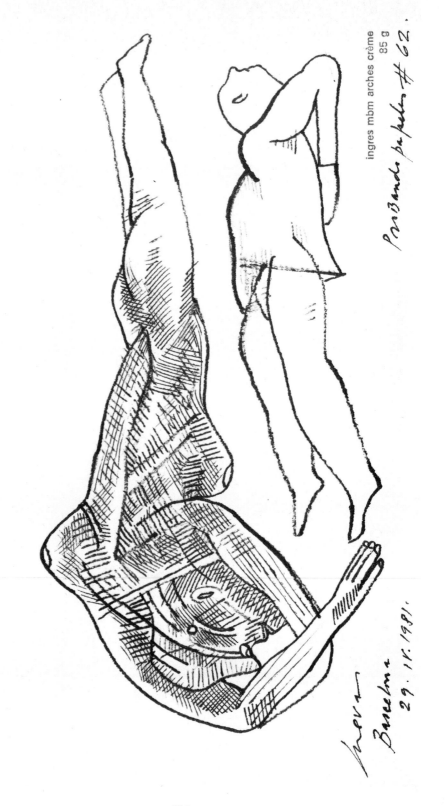

ingres mbm arches crème
85 g

Prssando papelon # 62.

Barcelona
29.IV.1981.

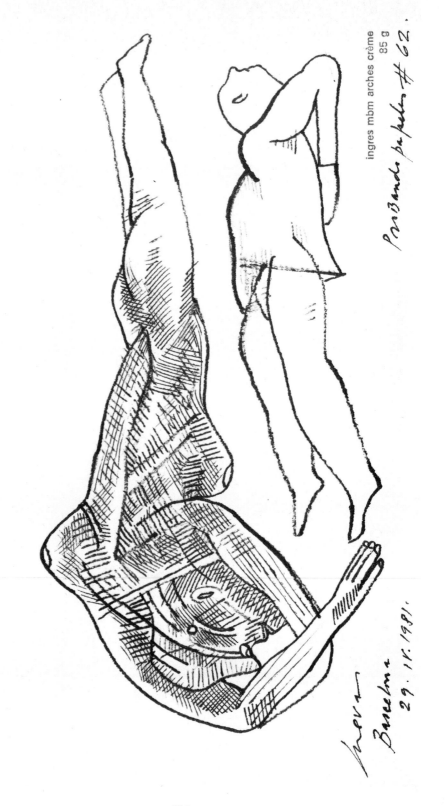

134

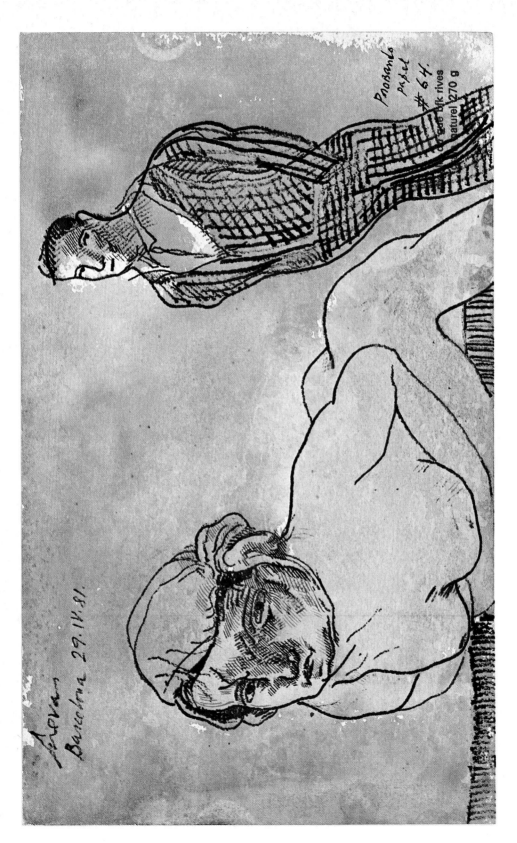

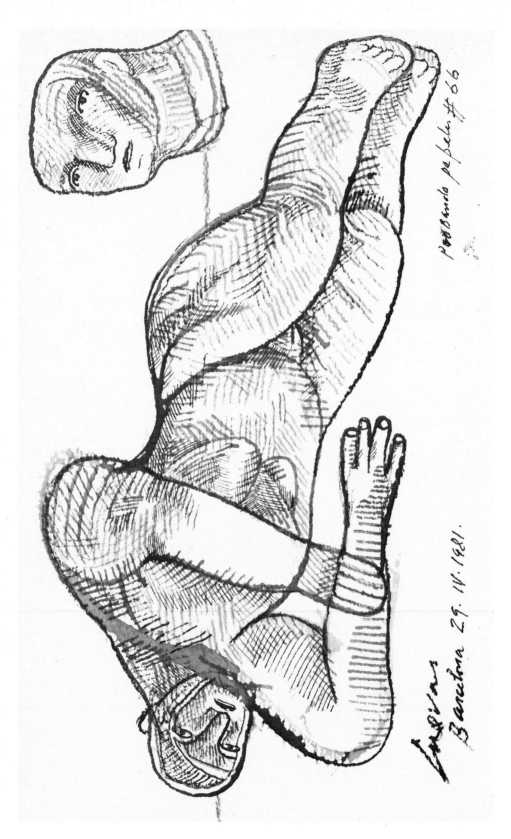

Pensando pa pela #66

Espinas
Barcelona 29. IV. 1981.

138

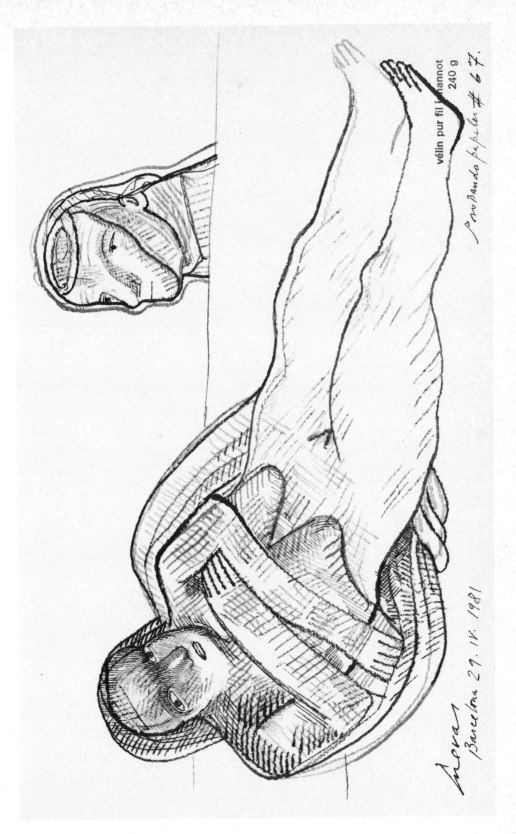

vélin pur fil channot
240 g

Probanda papeles # 67.

Moran
Barcelona 29. IV. 1981

aquarelle arches fin
300 g

Probando papels #68

Barcelona 29.IV.81

141

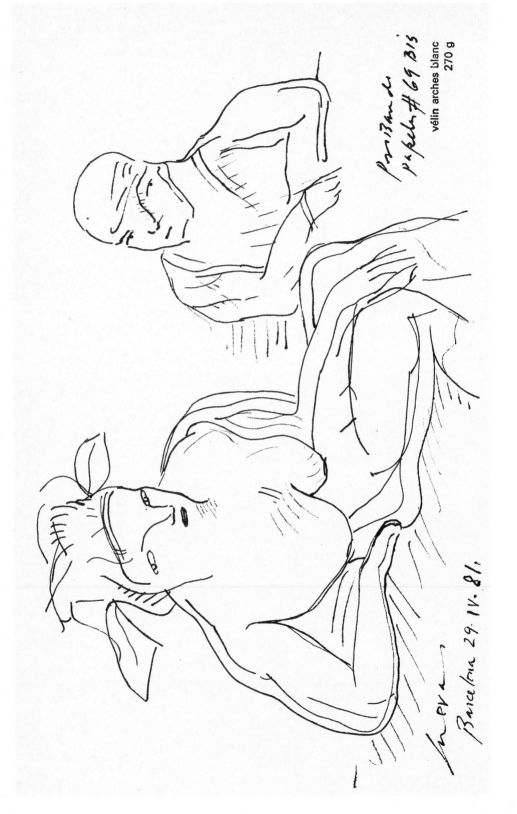

Pushmine
Papelong # 69 Bis
vélin arches blanc
270 g

Eva
Barcelona 29. IV. 81.

142

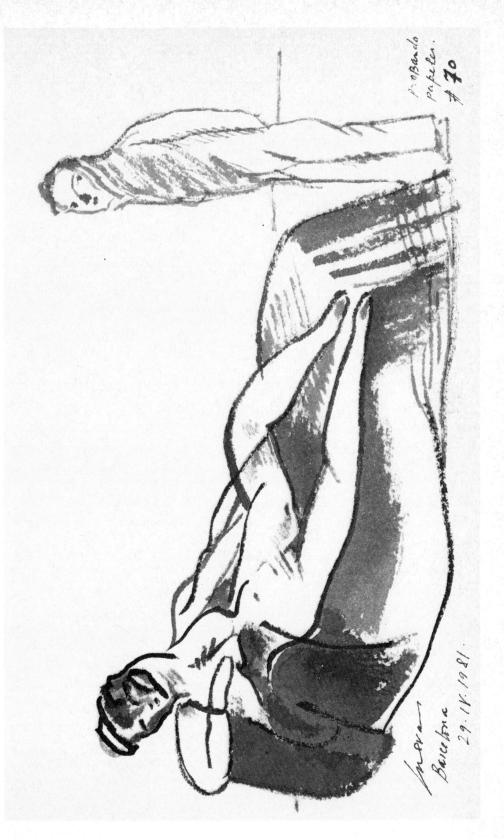

probando papeles
90 (bis)
aquarelle arches fin
640 g

Barcelona 29 IV. 81

144

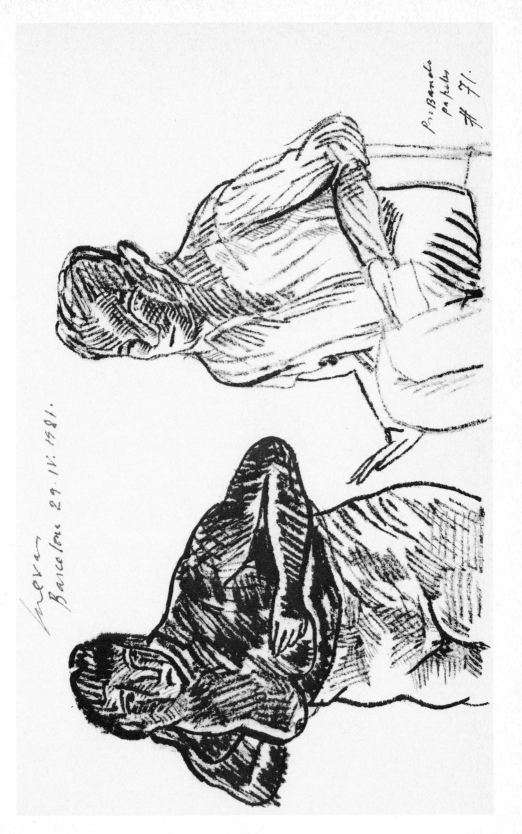

aquarelle arches torchon
300 g

146

aquarelle arches torchon
640 g

147

148

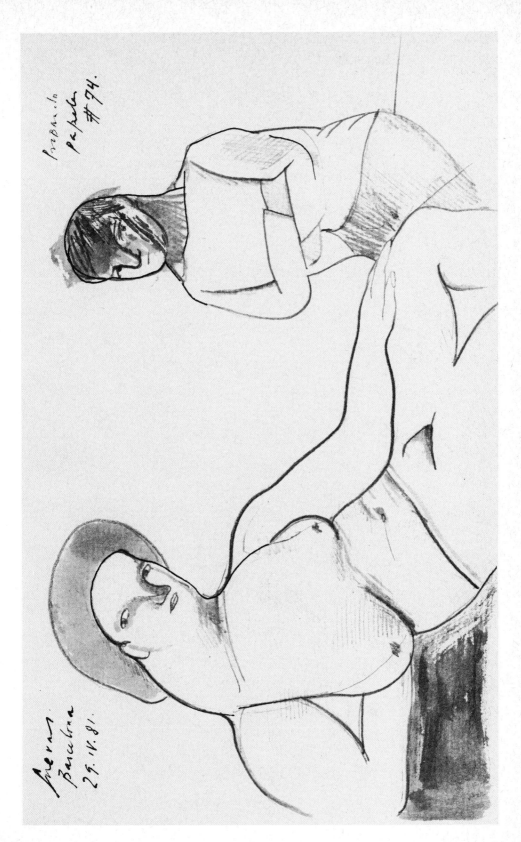

CHRONOLOGY

Born in Mexico City, in 1934

One-man shows

1948 First exhibition, at premises in the Calle de Donceles, Mexico City

1953 Galería Prisse, Mexico City

1954 Pan-American Union, Washington, D.C.

1955 Galerie Edouard Loeb, Paris

1956 Galería Proteo, Mexico City
Palace of Fine Arts, Havana

1957 Aenlle Gallery, New York

1958 Instituto de Arte Contemporáneo, Lima
Galería de Arte Contemporáneo, Caracas

1959 Galería Bonino, Buenos Aires

1960 Exhibition of 50 cards at the Galería Antonio Souza, Mexico City
David Herbert Gallery, New York
Silvan Simone Gallery, Los Angeles
Retrospective exhibition at the Art Center, Fort Worth, Texas

1961 Galleria l'Obelisco, Rome
Retrospective exhibition at the University of Austin, Texas
Santa Barbara Museum, Santa Barbara, California

1962 Galleria Sixtina, Milan
Jerrold Morris International Gallery, Toronto
Occidental College, Toronto

1963 Retrospective exhibition of the artist's graphic work at the
Pan-American Union, Washington, D.C.
Andrew Morris Gallery, New York
288 Gallery, St Louis, Missouri
Galería Antonio Souza, Mexico City

1964 Galleria Profili, Milan
Silvan Simone Gallery, Los Angeles
Biblioteca Luis Angel Arango, Bogotá

1965 Grace Borgenicht Gallery, New York
William Munson Proctor Institute, Museum of Utica, New York
Homage exhibition, entitled "Cuevas before Cuevas," at the
Galería Mer-Kup, Mexico City

1966 Galería Misrachi, Mexico City
Silvan Simone Gallery, Los Angeles

1967 Grace Borgenicht Gallery, New York

1968 Walter Engel Gallery, Toronto
Twenty galleries in the United States

1969 Glade Gallery, New Orleans

1970 Galería Misrachi, Mexico City
San Francisco Museum of Art, San Francisco
Homage exhibition at the University Museum of the University City,
Mexico City

1971 Grace Borgenicht Gallery, New York
Sala Nacional de Exposiciones, San Salvador
Galería El Morro de San Juan, Puerto Rico
Museo de Bellas Artes, Toluca, Mexico

1972 Michael Wyman Gallery, Chicago
Six Humbold Galleries in the United States
Museo de Arte Moderno, Mexico City

1973 Rothman Galleries, Toronto
Museo de Arte Moderno, Bogotá
Galería Aele, Madrid
Galería Pecanins, Barcelona

1974 Palais de Beaux-Arts, Brussels
Galería Multipla, São Paulo
Museo de Arte Contemporáneo, Caracas

1975 Museum of Fine Arts, San Diego, California
Art Museum, Phoenix, Arizona
Palace of the Legion of Honor, San Francisco
Fullerton College, Los Angeles
Individual room at the Biennale of São Paulo
Museum of Modern Art, Göteborg, Sweden
National Museum, Warsaw

1976 Museo de Arte Moderno, Mexico City
Sindin Gallery, New York
Retrospective exhibition at the Musée d'Art Moderne de la Ville de Paris,
Paris
ART 76, Basel

1977 Galería Estudio Actual, Caracas
Room of honor at the exhibition "Contemporary Art in Latin America",
Museo de Arte Moderno, Madrid
Retrospective exhibition at the Musée des Beaux-Arts, Chartres
Galería Misrachi, Mexico City
Galerie de Seine, Paris

1978 Ludwig Museum, Cologne
Grace Borgenicht Gallery, New York
Homage of the Organization of American States in Washington, D.C.
Exhibition at the Museum of Latin-American Art

1979 Museo de Arte Moderno, Mexico City
Tasende Gallery, San Diego, California

1980 Retrospective exhibition at the Museum of Monterrey, Mexico

1981 Meeting-Point Gallery, Miami, Florida
"Signos de Vida", Galería Kin, Mexico City

Museum of Ponce, Puerto Rico. Works by Cuevas in collections in
Puerto Rico
Pape Library-Museum, Monclova, Mexico
Galería Sloane Racotta, Mexico City

1982 Galería Joan Prats, Barcelona
Galerie Michel Delorme, Paris
Galería de Arte Mexicano, Mexico City
Galería Juan Martín, Mexico City
Galería Mer-Kup, Mexico City
Galería Sloane Racotta, Mexico City
Galería Pecanins, Mexico City
Galería José María Velasco, Mexico City
Museo de la Antigua Escuela de Medicina, Mexico City
Claustro de Sor Juana Inés, Mexico City
Centro Cultural de la Secretaría de Hacienda, Mexico City
Librería M. A. Porrúa, Mexico City
Tasende Gallery, La Jolla, California
Meeting Point Gallery, Miami, Florida
Galería Yvonne Briceño, Lima
Latin-American Art Museum, Washington, D.C.

Some group shows

1957 "Quatre maîtres de la ligne," Musée de la Napoule, France, with Alexander
Calder, Stuart Davis and Morris Graves.

1967 Selected to participate in "Rosc 67", Dublin. This edition of Rosc is entitled
"The fifty most important painters of the last four years".

1970 Exhibition of works by Cuevas and other artists, belonging to the José
Gómez-Sicre Collection, at the College Art Gallery, New Platz, New York.

1972 International Engraving Exhibition at the Venice Biennale.
Fundación Mendoza, Caracas, with works by Francisco Goya and Larry Rivers.

1975 Exhibit of 30 works, representing Galería Aele of Madrid, at the International
Exhibition, Basel.

1978 Salon de Mai, Paris.
FIAC, Grand Palais, Paris.
Documenta, Kassel, Germany.

1980 FIAC, Grand Palais, Paris.

Prizes

1959 International First Prize for Drawing at the São Paulo Biennale, with 40
works from the series *Funeral of a Dictator*.

1962 International First Prize at the "7th International Black and White
Exhibition," Lugano, Switzerland.

1964 Prize for Excellence in Art and Design at the 29th Annual Exhibition of the Art Directors' Club, Philadelphia.

1965 Madeco Prize at the 2nd Biennale Santiago de Chile.

1967 Annual Scenography Prize for his work on *La noche de los asesinos,* Mexico City.

1968 International First Prize for Engraving at the 1st Triennale, New Delhi.

1977 First Prize at the 3rd Biennale of Latin-American Engraving, San Juan, Puerto Rico.

1978 First Prize at the Stuttgart Book Festival, for *Cuaderno de París.*

1981 National Prize for Fine Arts, Mexico.

BIBLIOGRAPHY

Books illustrated by José Luis Cuevas

1. *Special editions with works by José Luis Cuevas*

The World of Kafka and Cuevas, Falcon Press, Philadelphia, 1959.
Recollections of Childhood, Kanthos Press, Los Angeles, California, 1962.
Cuevas-Charenton, Tamarind Workshop, Los Angeles, California, 1966.
Crime by Cuevas, Touchstone Publishers, Ltd., New York, 1968.
Homage to Quevedo, Collectors Press, San Francisco, California, 1969.
Cuevas Comedies, Collectors Press, San Francisco, California, 1972.
La Rue des Mauvais Garçons, Imprimerie Clot. Bransen et Georges, Paris, 1972.
Cuaderno de París, Multiarte, Mexico City, 1977.
Ritratti ed autoritratti, Zarathustra, Milan, 1979.

2. *Other books illustrated*

The ends of legends string, by William McLeod, Views Associates Press,
 Washington, D.C., 1960, illustrated with ten drawings.
Las citas, by Manuel Moreno Jimeno, La Rama Florida, Lima, 1960, illustrated
 with five drawings.
Los hombres y las cosas sólo querían jugar, Editorial Ecuador 0°00'',
 Mexico City, 1962, illustrated with five drawings.
Teatro Pánico, by Alexandro Jodorowsky, Ediciones Era, Mexico City, 1965,
 illustrated with twenty drawings.
El corno emplumado (review), Sergio Mondragón and Margaret Randall, Mexico,
 April 1966, illustrated with 20 drawings.
La siesta, Editorial Jorge Alvarez, S. A., 1967, cover illustration.
Poesía secreta, by Alfonso de Neuvillate, Mexico, 1967, cover illustration.
Espigas abiertas, by J. Ruiz Dueñas, Editorial Ecuador 0°00'', Mexico City,
 1968, illustrated with five drawings.
A principio de cuentas, by Francisco de Asís Fernández, Editorial Ecuador 0°00'',
 Mexico City, 1968, illustrated with one drawing.
Conte pour enfants de moins de trois ans, by Eugene Ionesco, booklet published
 by the Organizing Committee of the 19th Olympic Games, Mexico City, 1968,
 illustrated with nine drawings.
After the storm, by Joseph Sommers, University of New Mexico Press, New Mexico,
 1969, illustrated with one drawing.
Mis malos niños, by Rivke Rosenfeld, Costa-Amic, Mexico City, 1969, cover
 illustration.
Borges, par lui-même, by E. Rodríguez Monegal, Editions du Seuil, Paris, 1970,
 two illustrations.
Argón 18 inicia, by Edmundo Domínguez Aragonés, Edit. Diógenes, Mexico, 1971,
 cover illustration.
Todos juntos, by Armando Guerra, Edit. Novara, S. A., Mexico City, 1971,
 cover illustration.
Ecocidio: la destrucción del medio ambiente, by Armando Cesarman,
 Joaquín Mortiz, Mexico City, 1972, cover illustration.
Sólo a dos voces, by Octavio Paz and Julián Ríos, Edit. Lumen, Barcelona, 1973,
 one illustration.
Donde el agua es blanca como el gis, by Edmundo Domínguez Aragonés,
 Ed. Diana, Mexico, 1973 (Novelistas Mexicanos, 17), cover illustration.

Memorias do medo, by Edla Van Steen, Ediçoes Melhoramentos, São Paulo, 1974,
   six illustrations.
"La copertina di José Luis Cuevas," in *Verso il 2000,* Quarto Mondo,
   Rome, 1975, cover illustration.
Cuentos a Orfeo, By Héctor Gally, Ed. Pax-México, Mexico City, 1976, illustrated
   with one drawing.
A redefinition of the resting state of the myocardial, by Eduardo Cesarman
   and Norman Brachfeld, Edit. Pax-México, Mexico City, 1976, cover illustration.
"Temas autorretratos," in *Escandalar,* Vol. 1, No. 4 (October-December 1978).
   Escandalar Inc., New York, 1978, illustrations.
Auguste Bolte, by Kurt Schwitters, Editions Galilée, Paris, 1960, illustrations.
Juan Rulfo, homenaje nacional, INBA/SEP, Mexico, 1980, illustrated with drawings.
Tierra final, by J. Ruiz Dueñas, Federación Editorial Mexicana, Mexico City, 1981,
   cover illustration.
Argil (XXIII-XXIV), Maeght Editeur, Paris, 1981, illustrated with eight drawings.

Books written by José Luis Cuevas

Cuevas por Cuevas, Ediciones Era, Mexico City, 1965.
Cuevario, Editorial Grijalbo, Mexico City, 1973.
Cuevas contra Cuevas, (in the press).

Principal books on José Luis Cuevas

José Luis Cuevas, with texts by Jean Cassou, Philippe Soupault and
   H. Flores Sánchez, Michel Brient Éditeur, Paris, 1955.
José Luis Cuevas, by Carlos Valdés, Ediciones de la UNAM, Mexico City, 1967.
El Mundo de José Luis Cuevas, by Carlos Fuentes, Ediciones de la Galería Misrachi,
   Mexico City, 1969.
Confesiones de José Luis Cuevas, by Alaíde Foppa, Fondo de Cultura Económica,
   Mexico City, 1975.
Revelando a José Luis Cuevas, by Daisy Ascher, Madero, Mexico City, 1979.
Cuevas: Ipotesi per una lettura, by Roberto Sanesi, Zarathustra, Milan, 1979.
Cartas para una exposición (Illustrated letters and poems dedicated to José Luis
   Cuevas), Universidad Autónoma Metropolitana, Unidad Azcapotzalco,
   Cuadernos Temporales, No. 4, Mexico City, 1981.
Les obsessions noires de José Luis Cuevas, with texts by Cuevas and by several
   European and Latin-American writers. Editions Galilée, Paris, 1981.
Letters, Tasende Gallery Editions, La Jolla, California, 1982.

Others books mentioning or reproducing works by José Luis Cuevas

The insiders, by Selden Rodman, Louisiana State University Press, 1960.
La pintura nueva en Latinoamérica, by Marta Traba, Ediciones Librería Central,
   Bogotá, 1961.
México pintura activa, by Luis Cardoza y Aragón, Ediciones Era, Mexico City, 1961.
El arte contemporáneo, esplendor y agonía, by Ida Rodríguez Prampolini,
   Editorial Pormaca, S.A. de C.V., Mexico City, 1964.
La pintura moderna mexicana, by Justino Fernández, Editorial Pomarca, S.A.
   de C.V., Mexico City, 1964.

Tientos y diferencias, by Alejo Carpentier, Ediciones de la UNAM, Mexico City, 1964.

El expresionismo en la plástica mexicana de hoy, by Margarita Nelken, Ediciones del INBA, Mexico City, 1964.

Drawings of the masters (II), by Una E. Johnson, Shorewood Publishers, New York, 1965.

Los cuatro monstruos cardinales: Bacon, Cuevas, Dubuffet y De Kooning, by Marta Traba, Ediciones Era, Mexico City, 1965.

The emergent decade, by Thomas Messer, Cornell University Press, 1966.

Charlas con pintores, by Jacobo Zabludovsky, Editorial Costa-Amic, Mexico City, 1966.

Homenaje a Justino Fernández, by Luis Garrido *et al,* Editorial Libros de México, S.A., Mexico City, 1966.

Artist's proof ("The annual of contemporary prints"), The Pratt Center for Contemporary Printmaking, in cooperation with Barre Publishers, New York, 1967.

Recuento para recuerdo, by Carmen Rosenzweig V, Published by José Yurrieta Valdés, Toluca, Mexico, 1967.

Pintura ¿moderna?, by Luis Quintanilla, Editorial Novaro, S.A., Mexico City, 1968.

Painter's workshop, by Leonard Brooks, Van Nostrand Reinhold Company, New York, 1969.

El surrealismo y el arte fantástico de México, by Ida Rodríguez Prampolini, Ediciones de la UNAM, Mexico City, 1969.

Contemporary art in Latin America, by Gilbert Chase, The Free Press, New York, 1970.

Casa con dos puertas, by Carlos Fuentes, Editorial Joaquín Mortiz, Mexico City, 1970.

Días de guardar, by Carlos Monsiváis, Ediciones Era, Mexico City, 1970.

Art in Latin America, by Gilbert Chase, The Free Press, New York, Collier Macmillan, London, 1970.

Law and order reconsidered, by David P. Stang *et al,* Bantam Editions, New York, 1970.

Pintura, verdad y mito, conversaciones con Camps Rivera, by Francisco Cabrera, Editorial Libros de México, S.A., Mexico City, 1971.

La polvere e il giaguaro, by Roberto Sanesi, Palazzo Editore, Milan, 1972.

Humanism in 20th-century art, by Barry Schwartz, Preager Publishers, New York, 1972.

Printmaking today, by Jules Heller, Holt, Rinehart and Winston, Inc., New York, 1972.

En el aire, by Jacobo Zabludovsky, Editorial Novaro, S.A., Mexico City, 1973.

Contemporary prints, by Rivalis Tloman, The Viking Press, New York, 1973.

Cara a cara II, by James R. Fortson, Ediciones Grijalbo, S.A., Barcelona, Buenos Aires, Mexico, 1973.

Dos décadas vulnerables en las artes plásticas latinoamericanas: 1950-1970, by Marta Traba, Editorial Siglo XXI, Mexico City, 1973.

La gravure contemporaine depuis 1942, by Riva Castleman, Office du Livre, Friburg, Switzerland, 1973.

Contemporary prints, by Riva Castleman, The Viking Press, Inc., New York, 1973.

Pintura contemporánea de México, by Luis Cardoza y Aragón, Ediciones Era, Mexico City, 1974.

Aventura plástica de Hispanoamérica, by Damián Bayón, Fondo de Cultura Económica (Col. Breviarios, No. 233), Mexico City, 1974.
América Latina en sus artes, by Damián Bayón, Editorial Siglo XXI, Mexico City, 1974.
Una década de crítica de arte, by Ida Rodríguez Prampolini, Editorial SEP Setentas, Mexico City, 1974.
Los signos de vida, by Marta Traba, Fondo de Cultura Económica, Mexico City, 1976. (Testimonios del Fondo).
Claves del arte actual, by Rafael Squirru, Editorial Troquel, Buenos Aires, 1976.
México arte moderno II, by Alfonso de Neuvillate Ortiz, Ediciones Galería de Arte Misrachi, Mexico City, 1975.
El artista latinoamericano y su identidad, by Damián Bayón, Monte Avila Editores, Caracas, 1977.
Dibujo en México, Instituto Latinoamericano de la Comunicación Educativa, Mexico City, 1978.
In/Mediaciones, by Octavio Paz, Editorial Seix Barral, Barcelona, 1980.
Cara a cara III, by James R. Fortson, Juan Pablos Editor, Mexico City, 1980.
Travesía de la escritura, by Julieta Campos *et al,* Instituto Nacional de Bellas Artes, Mexico City, 1980.
Contemporary Mexican Painting in a Time of Change, by Shifra M. Goldman, University of Texas Press, Austin and London, 1981.
Arte de América 25 años de crítica, by Rafael Squirru, Ediciones Gagliarione, Buenos Aires, 1981.

Books providing biographical data on Cuevas

Who's Who in Graphic Art, Amsttuz and Herdeh, Graphic Press, Zürich, 1962.
Pintura actual México 1966, by Alfonso de Neuvillate, Ediciones de Arte de México y el Mundo, S.A., Mexico City, 1966.
Enciclopedia del Arte en América, Vol. I, Vicente Gesualdo *et al,* Bibliográfica Omeba, Buenos Aires, 1969.
Current Bibliography 1968 (Vol. 29), edited by Charles Mortiz, H. W. Wilson Company, New York, 1969.
Artists' Dictionary (American painters and sculptors), Mantie Fieldings Dictionary, James F. Carr Books, New York, 1969.
The International Who's Who, European Publications Limited, London (as from 1968-69).
Who's Who in the World, Marquis who's who, Inc., Chicago (as from 1971-72).
Who's Who in American Art, The Jaques Cattel Press, Tempe, Arizona, 1972.
A Visual Dictionary of Art, New York Graphic Society, New York, 1974.
Historia de México, Vol. 10, coordinated by Luis González, Salvat Editores de México, S.A., 1974.
Contemporary Artists, St. James Press, London, 1975.
American Printmakers, 75-76, Graphics Group, Arcadia, California.
Dictionnaire des peintres, sculpteurs, dessinateurs et graveurs, Vol. III. E. Benezit, Paris, 1976.
Artistas plásticos México 77, edited by Jorge D'Angeli, Ediciones Culturales GDA, Mexico City, 1977.
Enciclopedia de México, Vol. II, coordinated by Agustín Yáñez, Instituto de la Enciclopedia de México, Mexico City, 1977.

Diccionario de arte y artistas, by Peter and Linda Murray, Parramón Ediciones,
Barcelona, 1978.
The New Encyclopaedia Britannica (Macropaedia, Vol. 12), W. & H. Benton,
Publisher, Chicago, 1979.
Dictionary of International Biography 1980, International Biographical Centre,
Cambridge.
Who's Who in America 1980-1981, Marquis Who's Who, Chicago.
Diccionario Enciclopédico Salvat Universal, Vol. VII, Salvat Editores, Barcelona, 1981.

Stage, decor and costumes designed by Cuevas

1965   Decor for a television program directed by Alfonso Arau, Channel 2,
Mexico City.

1965   Decor for a musical show presented by Arau at the El Quid cabaret,
Mexico City.

1967   Decor for the play *La noche de los asesinos,* by José Triana, produced by
J. J. Gurrola at the Teatro Xola, Mexico City.

1968   Decor for the play *Retorno al hogar,* by Harold Pinter, produced by
J. J. Gurrola at the Teatro de los Insurgentes, Mexico City.

1970   Decor and costumes for the ballet *A Poem Forgotten,* with choreography by
Eliot Feld and music by Wallingford Riegger, American Dance Foundation,
Brooklyn Academy of Music, New York.

Films on Cuevas

José Luis Cuevas, by Juan José Gurrola, with texts by Ramón Xirau, Juan García
Ponce and José Luis Cuevas, spoken by Beatriz Sheridan and Claudio Obregón;
photography by Julio Pliego, Rafael Corkidi and Antonio Reynoso; music by
Raúl Cosío. (UNAM, 1964-66). 30 minutes. Mexico City.
José Luis Cuevas, by Alexandro Jodorowsky, with script by Jodorowsky; spoken by
José Luis Cuevas and Alexandro Jodorowsky; produced by Héctor Cervera.
1970. 30 minutes. Mexico City.
Cuevas Comedies, by William Wagner; script and montage by William Wagner;
produced by Collectors Press, San Francisco. 1971. 30 minutes.
José Luis Cuevas, by Graciela Iturbide, with script by Graciela Iturbide and Carlos
Hoyos; produced by CUEC. 1972. 30 minutes. Mexico City.
José Luis Cuevas, by Angel Hurtado, with texts by José Gómez-Sicre, spoken by
José Ferrer. (O.A.S., Washington, D.C.). 30 minutes. 1978.
José Luis Cuevas. Apuntes biográficos, by the Universidad Autónoma Metropolitana-
Azcapotzalco. 1981. 30 minutes. Mexico City.

Teaching activities

Professor of Drawing at the Art School of the Latin-American University,
Mexico City, 1956-57.
Artist in residence during the winter of 1977-78 at the Philadelphia Museum School
of Art, Philadelphia.

Guest artist at the Art School of San José State College, San José, California.
Guest artist at the Art School of Fullerton College, California.
Guest artist at the Art School of Washington University, Seattle.

Symposia

2nd Symposium organized by the Interamerican Foundation for the Arts, in
   Barranquitas, San Juan, Puerto Rico and New York, 1963.
3rd Symposium organized by the Interamerican Foundation for the Arts, in Mexico
   City and Mérida, Yucatán, 1964.
5th National Art Festival organized by the National Student Press Association,
   in Mérida, Yucatán, 1968.
International Youth Forum, at the Medical Centre, Mexico City, 1970.
Latin-American Art, at the University of Texas, Austin, Texas, 1975.

Lectures

Occidental College, Los Angeles
Institute of Contemporary Art, Lima
San Marcos Academy of Fine Arts, Lima
"Ver y Estimar" Group, Buenos Aires
Biblioteca Luis Angel Arango, Bogotá
Museum of Modern Art, Bogotá
University Precinct of Mayagüez, Puerto Rico
University of San Juan, Puerto Rico
Auditorium Caess, San Salvador
Colima University, Colima, Mexico
Regional Technological Institute, Oaxaca, Mexico
Technological Institute, Monterrey, Mexico
Guanajuato University, Guanajuato, Mexico
Yucatán University, Mérida, Yucatán
Teatro de la Paz, San Luis Potosí, S.L.P., Mexico
Ateneo Español, Mexico City
Mexican-Israeli Cultural Institute, Mexico City
Deportivo Israelita, Mexico City
Auditorium of the Cowdray British-American Hospital, Mexico City
Fashion Group, Mexico City
National Polytechnic Institute, Mexico City
La Casa del Lago, Mexico City
National Autonomous University of Mexico, Mexico City
San Carlos Academy, Mexico City
Latin-American University, Mexico City
Mexico City Museum, Mexico City
Tribuna de Pintores, Chapultepec, Mexico City
Auditorium of the National Museum of Anthropology and History, Mexico City
Museum of Modern Art, Mexico City
Monterrey Museum, Monterrey, N.L., Mexico
Loewe Museum, Miami, Florida

**Museums and institutions open to the public
which contain works by José Luis Cuevas**

Albi, France:	Toulouse-Lautrec Museum
Andover, Michigan:	Museum of the University of Michigan
Barranquilla, Colombia:	Museum of Barranquilla
Bogotá:	Biblioteca Luis Angel Arango
	Museum of Modern Art
Caracas:	Museum of Fine Arts
Cartagena, Colombia:	Museum of Cartagena
Chicago:	Art Institute of Chicago
Dallas, Texas:	Dallas Museum of Fine Arts
Jerusalem:	The National Museum of Bezalel
La Paz:	National Gallery
Lima:	Institute of Contemporary Art
Los Angeles:	Museum of the University of California
Lyons:	Museum of Fine Arts
Marseilles:	Museum of Fine Arts
Mexico City:	Museum of Modern Art
	Rufino Tamayo Museum of Contemporary Art
Milwaukee, Wisconsin:	Art Center of Milwaukee
New York:	Brooklyn Museum
	Museum of Modern Art
	Solomon R. Guggenheim Museum
Philadelphia:	Philadelphia Museum of Art
Phoenix, Arizona:	Phoenix Art Museum
San Diego, California:	Fine Arts Gallery of San Diego
São Paulo:	Museum of Modern Art
Santa Barbara, California:	Santa Barbara Museum of Art
Tel-Aviv:	The Museum of Art of Tel-Aviv
Toronto:	Art Gallery of Ontario
Utica, New York:	Munson-Williams-Proctor Institute
Washington, D.C.:	Hirshhorn Museum
	Pan-American Union Art Collection
	Phillips Collection
Worcester, Massachusetts:	Worcester Art Museum

All the drawings reproduced
in this book were carried out in Barcelona
on the sheets of a paper in the sample-book.
They were executed on the
27th and 29th of April 1981.